Carmichael Lewis Copyright © 2020 All Rights Reserved

All Rights Reserved. No part of this publication may be reproduced or transmitted in any form or by any means, mechanical or electronic, including photocopying and recording, or by any information storage and retrieval system, without permission in writing from the author or publisher (except by a reviewer, who may quote brief passages and/or show brief video clips in a review).

Disclaimer: The Publisher and the Author make no representation or warranties concerning the accuracy or completeness of the contents of this work and specifically disclaim all warranties for a particular purpose. No warranty may be created or extended through sales or promotional materials. The advice and strategies contained herein may not be suitable for every situation. This work is sold with the understanding that the Author and Publisher are not engaged in rendering legal, technological, or other professional services. If professional assistance is required, the services of a competent professional should be sought. Neither the Publisher nor the Author shall be liable for damages arising therefrom.

The fact that an organization or website is referred to in this work as a citation and/or potential source of further information does not mean that the Author or the Publisher endorses the information, the organization, or website it may provide or recommendations it may make. Further, readers should be aware that websites listed in this work may have changed or disappeared between when this work was written and when it is read.

Disclaimer: The cases and stories in this book have had details changed to preserve privacy.

Published by Writer's Publishing House
writerspublishinghouse.com

Paperback ISBN: 978-1-64873-221-8

Ebook ISBN: 978-1-64873-222-5

The Gold Mind
Mindset is Everything

By Carmichael Lewis

\gōld ˈmīnd\

:a mental state describing a person who has decided that nothing will alter their positive mindset.

a mental state describing a person who refuses to be defeated.

an invincible mindset.

TABLE OF CONTENTS

TABLE OF CONTENTS 4

INTRODUCTION 8

The Gold Mind 14

PART ONE 18

   HOW YOU THINK 18

      START EVERY DAY WITH GRATITUDE 18
      KEEP A POSITIVE ATTITUDE 20
      HEALTHY MIND, HEALTHY BODY 23
      ALWAYS CHOOSE POSITIVE 25
      OPTIMISM 27
      NEGATIVE THOUGHTS 30
      FIXED MINDSET vs. GROWTH MINDSET 34
      SELF-DISCIPLINE 40
      KNOW HOW VALUABLE YOU ARE 43
      FEEL GOOD ABOUT YOURSELF 45
      BELIEVE IN YOURSELF 47
      FIND YOUR HAPPINESS 50
      KNOW YOUR WHY 54
      BE YOUR OWN INSPIRATION 57

PART TWO 61

   WHAT YOU DO 61

PRACTICE SELF-CARE	61
GET CONFIDENT	65
SPEAK NICELY TO YOURSELF	69
WRITE DOWN WHAT YOU ARE GRATEFUL FOR	72
MAGNIFY YOUR STRENGTHS	75
LESSONS NOT LOSSES	77
TRANSITIONING	81
GIVING	84
VOLUNTEERING	87
SMILE MORE	89
OPEN YOURSELF UP TO HUMOR	91
MENTAL HEALTH	93
WORRYING	95
STRESS IS AN IDEA	97
MANAGE YOUR STRESS	99
THERAPY	101
MEDITATION	103
PICTURE MEMORY	105
JOURNALING	107
BE MINDFUL, NOT A MIND FULL	110
EXERCISE	112
PRACTICE WELLNESS TO PREVENT ILLNESS	113
WHAT ARE YOU WATCHING ON TV?	115
WHAT ARE YOU LISTENING TO?	117
WHO ARE YOU FOLLOWING?	120
INVEST IN YOURSELF	122
SETTING GOALS	124
TAKE ALL THE STEPS	128
PLAN FOR OBSTACLES	129

CHALLENGES	131
REWARD FOR SUCCESS	135
ORDINARY MOMENTS	137
TAKE IT AT A GRADUAL PACE	138
PROCRASTINATION	139
COMMUNICATION	141
SOCIAL ATTUNEMENT	145
WATCH YOUR WORDS	147
WHAT SUCCESS LOOKS LIKE	149
VISUALIZE SUCCESS	151
ACCOMPLISHMENTS	153
MOTIVATION	155
DO IT FOR MORE THAN MONEY	157
EQ VS. IQ	159
INTELLECT vs. INSTINCT	161
MONEY MANAGEMENT	163
PLAY THE OFFENSE	166
LEARN WHAT YOU CAN CONTROL	168
SET ALARMS ON YOUR PHONE	169
CHECK YOUR POSTURE	171
DECLUTTER YOUR LIFE	173
MAJOR VS. MINOR	175
TAKING THINGS PERSONALLY	177
TAKE THE HIGH ROAD	180
SEPARATE YOUR FEELINGS FROM YOUR PERFORMANCE	182
CYNICISM	185
IT'S OKAY TO SAY NO	188
CHOOSE JOY	190

BELIEVE IN YOURSELF 192
HUMAN BEING NOT HUMAN DOING 194
ENJOY THE PROCESS 196
GET UNCOMFORTABLE 198
EXPOSURE 200
NO MORE ZERO DAYS 203
NEXT LEVEL 205
ROUTINE 207
MIND YOUR OWN BUSINESS 209
ENCOURAGE, DON'T CRITICIZE 211
TAKE INVENTORY 213

PART THREE 215

YOUR GOLD CIRCLE 215

STAYING PRESENT 215
NO CRYING ALONE 217
NOT ME, BUT ME TOO 219
SURROUND YOURSELF WITH POSITIVE PEOPLE __ 222
WHO IS YOUR INFLUENCE? 225
GET A MENTOR 229
COACHING 231
CREATE YOUR MASTERMIND GROUP 234
ACCOUNTABILITY 236
EXPECTATIONS 238

Conclusion 239

INTRODUCTION

As a young man growing up in the inner city of Chicago, I lost complete control over my life. I was never a book-smart kid, and I made one stupid mistake after the other. I did every knucklehead thing you could think of. I hung out with the wrong crowd. I started skipping class. I got arrested. Anything that I could do to try my parents' patience, I did it. The guilt that I felt from making a series of wrong decisions began to weigh on my mind.

I began to doubt that the future I was capable of having was possible and that I would have to stay stuck in a life where everything around me was beneath me.

I believed that I would always be a victim of my circumstances.

It wasn't until my twenties that something clicked for me. I decided that I wanted—no, I needed—to turn my life around. I knew that if I made different decisions, followed by different actions, I could be better. In fact, I could be greater.

It took me years to learn the true power of a positive mindset. My shift didn't happen overnight, but, little by little, I took control of my life and improved myself mentally, physically, and even financially. Sure, I still had setbacks. But now I knew that I actually had the ability to control my thoughts, how I felt about myself, and how I showed up in the world. I learned that a bad day or bad situation didn't have to become a bad life. I learned that I could make mistakes, fail, and fall down—but I didn't have to stay down. I could keep going and growing. Every time I got back up after life knocked me down, I came back better, stronger, and greater.

I discovered a daily diet of information and motivation to feed my hungry mind. I stayed positive in the face of adversity. I kept supportive people around me. I created habits that helped me stay healthy, happy, and focused.

Today, I have a successful career in law enforcement. I am a motivational speaker and an author who inspires people all over the country. I am happily married with a loving family. All these achievements were once goals that felt out of reach. But my mind wouldn't allow me to give up on them.

I wrote this book to shorten the distance between where you are and where you want to be. You may want a life that looks completely different from mine, and that's fine. It doesn't matter what you want for yourself or what your vision of your life is. That's for you to decide.

Regardless of what you desire, what you want to do, or where you want to go, here's what I want you to know: You need a Gold Mind to get there.

And that's why I wrote this book.

***

I'm sure this is not the first personal development book you've ever picked up. Some of them you've probably skimmed through. Some of them you may have finished. Most of them you did not.

I want this to be a different experience for you.

This book was designed to guide you and be a reference that you come back to again and again.

More importantly, it was designed for you to actually do the work to change your mindset and your life.

This book is divided into three parts, with each one serving a unique purpose on your journey to a Gold Mind. The first focuses on your thoughts, the second on your actions, and the third on your environment. You'll need all three to make a real change in your life.

Do not try to digest this book in one sitting. Instead, set aside some time each day to read 1-2 of the practical principles in each section. Think about them. Apply them to your life. Adjust your mindset, step by step. I guarantee you will see significant changes over time. Because this book is focused on retraining your subconscious mind, you will notice that you will think and act differently, often without even realizing it. Positivity will become your default.

But the information in this book is only valuable to you if you apply it.

That's why each section includes actionable steps (Gold Mind Work) and reflections (Gold Mind Mantras) for you to apply to your daily life. I encourage you to take the work seriously and put these tools into practice.

If you do that, by the end of this book, you'll be equipped to live a more purposeful life. I'm not asking you to change your life completely or turn it upside down. I'm simply asking you to think about life in a different way. I'm asking you to be more *mindful*, instead of having a *mind full* of past mistakes, doubt, defeat, and failures. I am asking you to be willing to respond differently when you are challenged, frustrated, and want to give up. I am asking you to learn what tools you need to pull out of your toolkit (the practices you'll learn throughout this book) to get your head back in the game and refocus.

Keep an open mind while you navigate through these pages. This book has a lot to offer, but it's up to you how much you take from it.

So, congratulations! You've taken the first step toward mastering your mind! You've made the decision to become better than you've ever been before.

Greatness awaits you.

Now, let's continue your journey…

**Control your mind
Control your behavior
Control your destiny**

The Gold Mind

Our thoughts, along with our environment, shape everything about who we are and who we become.

When it comes to our day-to-day lives, we often regard situations as happening *to* us, instead of happening *for* us. But the truth is, everything we experience occurs for a reason. Sometimes it's to teach us. Sometimes it's to protect us. Every time, it's to remind us that nothing in our lives is a coincidence. Every day we get to choose the lens through which we look at ourselves and the world.

Positivity is a perspective.

Think about your drive to work. There's the traffic and the constant red lights between you and where you need to be in the next few minutes. You're running late and you feel rushed. You're irritated and you can feel your blood boiling. The mere thought of this might make you shudder.

But consider this: what if a terrible accident has occurred on the road ahead of you, and the traffic and red lights actually saved your life by making you late? What you thought was an inconvenience or the universe conspiring against you was really a lesson or protection. Either way, your mind gets to decide whether you see your delay as positive or negative.

How different would your life be if you shifted your mindset to see the good, or—better yet—the great, in every situation? What would happen if you decided today that life is not happening *to* you, it's happening *for* you?

We all have bad, even horrible, days. We all face challenges. Whether it's being stuck in traffic, losing a job, or not getting the big break we know we deserved, tough times happen. But every one of those scenarios could be setting us up for our next great win. If we can't push past what is attempting to stop us, we'll never know. That's why the key to lifelong success is to not allow what happens to us to throw us completely off course or to dictate the direction of our next steps. We have to learn how to keep going, no matter what.

This book will teach you how to do that.

Anyone who has ever run a marathon will tell you that their success was contingent upon consistent conditioning. While physical endurance plays a huge part in their performance, there is something far more important than that—the mind. It's the mind that keeps the body going, rain or shine. It's the mind that tells the legs not to give out or give in. It's the mind that moves the feet across the finish line.

You may not be a runner or dream of completing an actual marathon, but leveraging the power of a positive mindset is a skill that will serve you in any area of your life. Your goals, dreams, and the life that you envision for yourself demand a mindset that is conditioned to continue, to press forward, to stay positive, and, most importantly, to get to the finish line.

This is what The Gold Mind is all about.

Before we jump in, I want to point something out to you.

This book is far more about action than talk. This book is about doing *your* work. This book is big on personal accountability and taking intentional actions toward your goals.

Let's be honest. It's easy to blame life, our circumstances, and others for what we don't have.

I'm not saying life hasn't been rough for you. You may have odds stacked against you. People who decided that you won't win. You may be facing some tough times.

But think about this (and be honest):

Do you hold yourself accountable when you have a task to complete? Are you intentional when going after the things you want in life? What are you doing to challenge yourself? Are you able to recognize your worth and feel grateful for what you have?

Notice that none of these questions have anything to do with anyone else—except you. And if the answer to any of them is "no" or "nothing", don't worry. You're in the right place.

Keep reading.

PART ONE
HOW YOU THINK

START EVERY DAY WITH GRATITUDE

The morning is the most important part of your day. From the moment you open your eyes, everything that happens next determines how your entire day will flow. If you wake up stressed and frustrated before your feet hit the floor, you can't expect your day to be filled with ease, clarity, or control. Believe it or not, you *can* completely control the direction of your day. You *can* take your mind where you want it to go. A positive mind is a conscious decision.

While your first thought in the morning might be, *Ugh, I have to wake up!* it doesn't take a lot of effort to start your day differently. Instead think, *I get to wake up!* Do you see the difference?

When you think about how many people went to bed thinking they'd wake up and didn't, you can't help but be thankful that you have another day and another opportunity to breathe, connect with the people you care about, and choose to go after whatever it is that's in front of you.

Starting your day in a peaceful, gracious way sends positive messages to your subconscious mind and sets you up for a whole day of positive thinking and action.

When given a choice, go with gratitude. It beats negativity every time.

Gold Mind Work
1. When you wake up in the morning, what are your first thoughts?
2. What is at least one thing you are grateful for?
3. How can you change your morning mindset to start your day on a more positive note?

Gold Mind Mantras
- I am grateful that I got to wake up this morning.
- I have complete control over my mind today.
- I have so much to be grateful for.
- I am blessed beyond measure.

KEEP A POSITIVE ATTITUDE

A positive attitude means believing everything will turn out just fine. Having a positive attitude is essential to remain happy, and to progress through life, whether it's at work, in school, or at home. A positive attitude magnifies your accomplishments and not your failures. It helps you see the good in people, not the bad. It helps you see your obstacles as opportunities. A positive attitude equals positive thinking.

Adopting a positive attitude means you stop saying "I can't" and start saying "I can." Stop focusing on your failures (we'll talk more about this more later), or how bad you think your life is. Shift your attitude by focusing on all the things that are *right* in your life, not what's wrong.

We've all experienced difficult situations that we could justifiably be hurt and angry about. But it is possible to change our perspective and the way we think about those experiences. We have the power to change our perspective from negative to positive at any moment. We don't have to dwell in defeat. We can be mindful of how and where we focus our energy. What we think is who we become.

Of course, no matter how positive a person is, bad things do happen, and, as humans, we will slip sometimes and allow our minds to wander to a negative space. But over time, you can learn how to reel those thoughts in quickly. Your goal should be to have more positive thoughts than negative ones. And the wonderful thing about thinking positively is that it can be self-taught, though it does require practice and patience.

A positive attitude comes with many rewards, such as happy friends, family, and co-workers. You're probably thinking how can *you* change the attitude of others? But it's true! Think about that one person in your life who brings you joy and inspiration when you're with them. Why do they make you feel that way? How is it that they make you smile? What is it about them that you love so much? Just think if you were able to be that positive influence for someone else.

Positivity pays itself forward. It's a gift that keeps on giving. The more positive energy you have, the more you can share with others.

Gold Mind Work

1. Take a moment, close your eyes, and take three deep breaths. Open your eyes and smile. Remember, someone didn't get to do that this morning.

2. The next time you're thinking negatively, take a moment and think of a way you can transform that thought into a positive one.

3. Make it your goal to be a positive person that people want to hang around. Positivity is contagious.

Gold Mind Mantras
- ◊ My mind is filled with positive thoughts.
- ◊ My energy is positive, and my mind is too.

HEALTHY MIND, HEALTHY BODY

If a person has a negative mindset and their mental health is out of whack, chances are they have the physical health to match.

According to an article written by Adrienne Santos for Healthline.com, studies show that women who were optimistic had a lower risk of dying from major causes of death, including heart disease, stroke, infection, respiratory disease, and much more. While this particular article focused on women, men should take note too. Stress affects us all and what this article proves is that it doesn't start in the body—it starts in the mind. Science and statistics do not lie.

Think about the people in your own life. How many people do you know personally who have allowed negativity, anger, resentment, and bitterness affect their overall health and quality of life? Do they do far more cussing and complaining than striving and working toward their goals?

Now, think about this.

- ◊ How many of them also suffer from some other chronic ailment like diabetes or headaches?
- ◊ How many of them are always sick and tired?
- ◊ Do you see the connection?

Your body follows your mind. When you maintain a healthy mind, your body will become healthier too.

Gold Mind Work

1. How often do you find yourself in stressful situations?
2. How do you manage stress?
3. Do you notice that you feel physically drained when your life feels out of control and chaotic?

Gold Mind Mantras

- ◊ I understand that my mind and body are connected, so I will stay mentally healthy.
- ◊ I will keep my stress levels low so that I can keep my body healthy too.
- ◊ I owe it to myself to keep my mind and body healthy.

ALWAYS CHOOSE POSITIVE

Positive thinkers don't always think positively. When something negative happens, they have a choice to make—to dwell in the doom or pick the positive. Those who are committed to living optimistically always choose the positive route.

Instead of staying stuck in everything that is going wrong, positive thinkers practice awareness and mindfulness. They stay present and understand that the situation is temporary.

They rarely label a thing as good or bad, right or wrong. Instead, they see every experience as an opportunity to learn something valuable, even if it's what *not* to do.

Be a positive thinker. Choose to rise above your circumstances and challenges, regardless of what happens around you or to you.

Gold Mind Work

1. Think about a hard situation that happened to you. What was it?
2. How did you respond to it? Did you see the experience as positive or negative at the time?

3. Looking back, can you see how the situation changed you for the better?
4. What lessons did you learn?

Gold Mind Mantras

- ◊ When faced with tough situations, I will stay in a positive frame of mind.
- ◊ Regardless of what happens to me, I will be stronger because of it.
- ◊ Life always works out in my favor.

OPTIMISM

Oftentimes, we think our way into negative thoughts and our thoughts become our reality. So, if this is true (which it is) why not think optimistically and create more positive results in our lives?

When we wake up each day, we have two options: optimism or pessimism. Whichever we choose sends a signal to our subconscious mind to either start looking for the good in things or to start looking for the bad in things. Whichever choice we make, our day will follow.

There are two types of people in this world: those who chose to think positively and those who don't. Both have control over not only their minds but the results that their thoughts create in their lives. Let me show you...

Let's take a look at Negative Nancy. She wakes up every morning and says, "Damn, I have to go to work." Nancy doesn't realize that she's sending negative signals to her brain. Now as she is preparing for work, everything is going bad. She spills coffee on her shirt. Rushing out of the door, she leaves her cellphone at home. As she's driving to the office, traffic is backed up. To make matters worse, she couldn't find parking and now she's late for work. Nancy's attitude caused her to have a negative morning.

On the other hand, Positive Patty is very optimistic. She wakes up before the alarm sounds and says, "Thank God, I have a job I get to go to." Patty sends positive signals to her brain so that she can see the good in things rather than the bad. Patty meditated before she goes to work, she had extra time to stop and get coffee, and, to her surprise, the man in front of her paid for her drink. She made it to work ahead of schedule and was able to find a parking spot. Because of Patty's positive energy and optimistic attitude, she was promoted to be a team leader to show others how to lead a positive life.

In these two examples, we see how we get to choose how we start our day and determine how our mindsets will impact the rest of the day, and, sometimes, our lives. We can either think our way into something good or into something bad.

Are you Negative Nancy or Positive Patty?

Be careful what you think. Look at what could happen instead of what won't happen. Become an optimistic thinker. It will change your day and your life.

Gold Mind Work

1. Are you more of an optimistic or pessimistic thinker?
2. How can you shift your thinking?

Gold Mind Mantra

◊ When given the opportunity to think positively or negatively, I will always choose positive.

NEGATIVE THOUGHTS

Negative thoughts are sneaky. Before you notice what's happening, they can creep in. And like a snowball, those thoughts keep building and building until they're completely out of control. What started as something small, like a bit of criticism from a co-worker or not getting a job you felt qualified for, turns into a lifetime failure in your mind. It's easy for one minor thing to become a major thing in our minds.

Negative thoughts are like untied shoelaces—they'll always trip you up. So, you have to catch them before they catch you and bring you down.

If a negative thought comes to mind, clear it out as quickly as possible. Replace that not-so-good thought with a positive one. Focus on the good things that happened today, like waking up, having a roof over your head, and being able to afford groceries to nourish your body. These are the things that truly matter.

But missed shots can sting too. So, if you missed an opportunity, think about how you can salvage it. Can you double back and correct? If not, plan now for how you can be better prepared next time. Another day and another chance will come your way, so focus on preparing for that chance as opposed to dwelling on the shots you've missed.

Trust me, I know what' it's like to feel like you "missed your shot." Let me take you back to when I failed the 6th grade. The thought of being left behind by my peers, being laughed at by friends, being called names, and repeating the same grade for another year is a lot of mental stress for a kid that age. Although I was not as mentally strong as I am now, something in me wouldn't allow myself to quit. I didn't drop out of school. I kept going.

My academic life didn't improve overnight and that wouldn't be my last setback. In high school, my GPA was 1.7. I never realized how important grades were until senior year when I was searching for colleges. I had to work diligently and intentionally to bring my GPA up. After hours of studying, I managed to graduate high school with a 2.7 GPA. At this point in my life, I was comfortable with failure because it caused me to dig my heels in deeper, read a little longer, and stay awake studying a little harder.

I made it to college and failed English three times. Though it was hard, I remembered what I learned from my past failures. I didn't quit. I knew I would make it. Never once did I allow my failure to become my future. I stayed resilient and continued to learn, focus, and persevere.

Because of those experiences, and many more after that, I can tell you to never give up on yourself or your dreams.

I'll say this a lot throughout this book, because I don't want you to forget it. When hard times come and you face failure or obstacles, look at the situation as another opportunity to understand it and yourself better.

Try harder. Learn from it. You'll be better for it.

When you catch your thoughts spiraling out of control and wanting to give up, get a hold of yourself. Reel your mind back in. Don't get caught drowning. Keep your head above water. Catch those negative thoughts and control them before they can control you.

Gold Mind Work

1. What are negative thoughts that you find yourself thinking constantly?
2. How can you turn those negative thoughts into positive ones?

Gold Mind Mantras

- ◊ I will be mindful of my thoughts.
- ◊ I am prepared for whatever comes my way.
- ◊ When life knocks me down, I bounce back quickly.
- ◊ I will not lose.

FIXED MINDSET vs. GROWTH MINDSET

Having a fixed mindset can be very harmful. A person with a fixed mindset believes they were born as they are and that's how they should live forever. They believe they can't or shouldn't do anything to improve themselves. Despite a world that is moving and evolving around them, they believe it's best to remain right where they are.

Here are a few ways you can identify if you have a fixed mindset:

You are resistant to new ideas or thinking. If you aren't open to learning new things or being exposed to people who think and live differently from you, chances are your mindset is fixed. When you have an opportunity to learn something new, have you ever said, "I'll stick with what I know"? (Don't worry. I was guilty of this too until I changed my thinking.)

You are completely comfortable in your life. When was the last time you were curious about something? It could be a new job, living in a different community or city, or starting a new hobby. If it's been *years*, there is a strong possibility your mind has limitations that need to be lifted.

You avoid challenges. This is a big one for a lot of people. How often do you give up on a difficult task? From losing a few pounds to studying for a test, if you tend to quit on the process and yourself before you reach your goal, your mindset needs to shift.

So, what does a growth mindset look like? I'm glad you asked...

You believe anything is possible. When you have a growth mindset, you believe that through hard work, dedication, and resilience, you can achieve anything. You aren't envious of other people's success, since seeing them win reminds you that you can do it too. You know there are no limits and big goals don't scare you. In fact, they fire you up.

Think about if you needed a new car, and, based on your bank account, the car you want is way out of reach. A person with a fixed mindset says, "I can't afford that car!" Someone with a growth mindset asks, "How can I afford that car?"

See the difference?

You crave positive change. Someone with a growth mindset is constantly looking for ways to learn, grow, and improve. You will be content and grateful for what you have, but there is a part of you that always wonders if there is more.

When you have a growth mindset, you want to expand and learn new things. You consider new ideas without shutting them down, and you try new things.

You run toward challenges instead of away from them. Challenges help us build confidence and to grow in unfamiliar areas. Giving up is the easiest thing to do, it takes no effort. When you have a growth mindset, you don't see challenges, you see opportunities. You seek failure because you know success is on the other side. When you make mistakes or receive criticism, you see it as a chance to learn.

The growth mindset refuses to give up. The growth mindset is dedicated and focused on the end goal. The growth mindset sees the desired destination and refuses to stop until it gets there.

I want you to develop a growth mindset (and I am here to help you) because that is how you become the best version of yourself. But you have to see how it can change your life

Can you achieve everything you want? Can you catch all the dreams you've been chasing? Can you have a bigger and brighter future?

If there is any part of you that hesitated to answer any of those questions, I'm here to tell you….

YOU CAN DO ALL THINGS.

I hope you begin to believe that. Shifting your mindset using the tools and practices in this book takes work. But I promise you that it's possible. You may have started this book unsure about what it would take to start changing your life. By now, I believe you are beginning to see what can happen for you if you are willing to do the work.

YOU CAN DO ALL THINGS.

You can change your mind. You can change your body. You can learn new things. You can have the success, income, and happiness you desire. Don't count yourself out. Don't give up.

YOU CAN DO ALL THINGS.

Repeat these words as often as you can until they become who you are.

Your mind wants to open, expand, and grow. You just need to allow it.

Gold Mind Work

1. What new things have you learned lately? What new ideas have you thought of? How have you opened your mind recently?

2. What are you doing to enhance your potential and reach your goals?

3. What steps are you taking that will lead you in the right direction?

Gold Mind Mantras

◊ I can do all things.

◊ Change will make me happier, help me reach my goals, and allow me to have the life I've always dreamed about.

SELF-DISCIPLINE

It is impossible to reach your goals without discipline. Everything that you want is on the other side of the hard choice to delay what feels and looks good *now* for what will be greater later.

If you want your dreams to come true, you can't just wish for them. You have to work for them.

Discipline makes the difference.

Discipline is the difference between sticking to a clean diet and unnecessarily eating food when we're full. Discipline is sticking to our word and doing the things we've said we're going to do, even if we don't particularly want to do it. Discipline is getting out of your warm, cozy bed to do a workout, even when it's cold, gloomy and raining.

After you've had a hard week and you want to unwind with a delicious cocktail, discipline reminds you not to have too many drinks and stops you from getting absolutely wasted. If you're saving for a house, discipline prevents you from buying that new car you want, even though you could probably afford it, but buying it will set you back months in your efforts to save. Discipline is performing well in the workplace, even though you're constantly overlooked for a raise or promotion. You still show up, and you get the job done, arriving early and staying late.

Here is the point: there is nothing you want that will not require you to choose to do what it takes to have it. There will always be something easier, more comfortable, more attractive than the work it takes to achieve your goals. You have to choose the work.

Discipline is rarely the easy choice. But it's always the necessary one.

Gold Mind Work
1. In what areas of your life do you need more discipline?
2. What would be the reward of becoming more disciplined in that area? How will your life improve?
3. What is one thing that you can do today to become more consistent toward that goal?

Gold Mind Mantras
- ◊ I can do anything I put my mind to.
- ◊ What seems hard is easy for me.

◊ I can do whatever is necessary to achieve my goals.

KNOW HOW VALUABLE YOU ARE

You are irreplaceable. You are a rare breed. The odds of finding someone exactly like you is one in a trillion. Remember that.

You bring value into every room you walk into. It could be your intelligence, your creativity, your giving heart, your ability to teach others, or all the above.

What seems small, easy, and natural to you is the missing piece to someone's success puzzle. It matters. Take inventory of what you offer and understand how valuable it is. Identify your core competencies and capitalize on them.

I once heard a great man, Jim Rohn, say that you get back the value you bring. Your value has a boomerang effect. When you give value, you get value back in return. Good things always come back to you in some form. Expect it.

Value also extends beyond the workplace. You bring value to your family, your marriage, and your relationships. Become a person of value in every area of your life.

Gold Mind Work

1. What do you do incredibly well?
2. What do people praise you for?
3. What value do you contribute (complete all that apply):
    a. At work and/or school?
    b. In your family?
    c. In your church?
    d. In your community?
    e. In your business?

Gold Mind Mantras

◊ I am valuable.
◊ I improve the lives of people wherever I go.
◊ There is no one who can do what I do, the way I do it.
◊ I am irreplaceable.

FEEL GOOD ABOUT YOURSELF

A positive point of view in life has a lot to do with how you feel about yourself. When you don't feel good about yourself, it's impossible to show up in the world, go for your goals, and give life all that you've got.

Knowing your self-worth brings a sense of confidence with it. How do you feel about yourself? Do you know what makes you special? Do you know that you are loved and cared about? Do you know you can achieve anything that you set your mind to?

All these things are true. When you know it and believe it, you can move in the world with your head held high, unstoppable.

If you find yourself in a negative thought pattern, check your thoughts. Eliminate self-criticism from your mind. When you look in the mirror, what is the first thing that comes to mind? If you can't look in the mirror and find something positive to say to yourself, it's time to change your thinking. Remind yourself who you are. This should be a daily practice.

Next, check your body language. Every day, make a mental note of how you feel and how those feelings affect how you show up. What attitude are you presenting? Are you smiling? Are your shoulders back and head held high?

How you carry yourself tells the world exactly how you feel about yourself. It's important to manage your perception. But first, you need to manage your mind.

You are exceptional. You are amazing. Know it. Feel it. And never forget it. YOU ARE SOMEONES REPLACEMENT!

Gold Mind Work
1. What do you love most about yourself?
2. When do you feel your best? How do you look?
3. Do you believe people have a positive or negative perception of you?
4. If you believe the perception is negative, how can you change that?

Gold Mind Mantras
- ◊ I love myself and everything about me.
- ◊ When people see me, they only see positivity.

BELIEVE IN YOURSELF

How often do you tell yourself, *yes, I can*? Take a moment now, before you keep reading, and say the words: YES, I CAN!

Think about any obstacles you're facing and say it again: YES, I CAN!

Think about anything that feels impossible to achieve right now and say it again: YES, I CAN!

YOU CAN AND YOU WILL.

As a teenager, I had so many ideas and dreams, from owning my own business to becoming a police officer, but I never really believed I could do any of them. My self-esteem, past mistakes, failures, where I lived, and who I spent the most time with all negatively influenced what I perceived my possibilities to be. My mind was full of so many doubts and self-imposed restrictions that I couldn't see past my present. To me, my future held nothing but more failures.

Like many people, I wanted to blame others for what I hadn't accomplished. Often, I'd share my dreams and ideas with friends and family, but, instead of support, all I received was negative feedback and doubts.

People would laugh when I told them my dreams, but, looking back, I couldn't blame them. How could I expect them to believe in something that I couldn't?

As I got older, it finally clicked that something needed to shift. I realized that *I* was the one standing in my own way. My own thoughts were limiting me. It didn't matter who else believed in me. What mattered most was that I believed in myself.

Fast forward to now, and I understand that it takes much more than a dream to make things a reality. Once I changed the way I thought, my habits and everything in my life followed. I became a new person. I started setting my goals and reaching them before the target date.

Self-belief is one of the most powerful tools you can possess. When you believe that you can achieve anything, big or small, nothing or no one can stand in your way. If you believe it, you can see it. And if you can see it, you can achieve it.

Have you heard the saying, "Positive thinking leads to positive outcomes"? It's true. Your Reticular Activating System, or RAS, helps you seek out information that validates your beliefs. If you think you are bad at public speaking, you probably will be. If you believe you're a hard worker, you most likely are. The RAS helps you see what you want to see and, in doing so, influences your actions. You are what you think.

Program your mind to believe that you can achieve anything. Believe it even before you see it.

Gold Mind Work
1. What is a dream that you want to achieve that feels far-fetched to you?
2. When would you like to achieve it? Within the next month? Next year? Five years?
3. What goals would it take for you to make that dream a reality?
4. What are the first three steps you can take (big or small) to move you in the direction toward your dream?

Gold Mind Mantras
- ◊ I believe in myself.
- ◊ I believe in my dreams.
- ◊ My dreams will become my reality.

FIND YOUR HAPPINESS

Happiness is a feeling of fulfillment. Sometimes, we achieve it by doing work we love. Other times, happiness comes from doing something we love alone or alongside people with whom we enjoy spending time. Happiness means different things for all of us. The key to maintaining a positive outlook on life is to ensure we have happiness—and plenty of it.

Far too often, we look to others to determine who we should be, what we should do, and what we should have. It's fine to be inspired and motivated by others' success. In fact, sometimes, we need to use other people's accomplishments to show us what's possible and to light a fire under our own potential, especially when our exposure is limited.

We all need tangible examples of what our lives could look like if we can escape our current environment and breathe new air. But we should never allow someone's else idea of happiness to trump the happiness that we want for ourselves. This includes people who love you most, like your parents.

Let me tell you a little story about parent-pleasing.

I decided to become a police officer to make my father proud. Growing up, he would always speak so highly of his friends who were on the force. With eager ears, I listened to story after story about the officers he knew. The look in his eyes and the pride in his voice made me want to do whatever I needed so that, one day, he would feel the same way about me. I craved that validation and support from him.

My mind started to devise a plan. I pursued the force with everything I had until I got there. Against so many odds, I finally got that badge. But I never got the praise from my father that I prayed would come with it.

My plan to finally have my father's approval did not work, and I am okay with it.

Don't get me wrong, the joy I get from helping the hungry, protecting kids and elders, supporting teenagers who were a lot like me as a kid, and giving the community a voice is very rewarding. But this may not have been the career I chose for myself. I'm living in someone else's dream, not my own.

I never gave myself an opportunity to discover my purpose and what happiness looked like for me. I've been a police officer for more than ten years, and now, I am discovering my *why*. I am deciding how I want my life to look and feel, and how I want to show up in the world and serve.

Here's the moral of the story: find and follow your own path to happiness and purpose.

Yes, you may want to make your family proud, but your priority is to make yourself proud by living a life that *you* love. You have to define and pursue your own happiness like your life depends on it—because it does.

Your life is yours for a reason. Your happiness doesn't have to be approved or understood by anyone else. People will doubt you. They will be disappointed that you are doing something different than what they want for you. Do it anyway.

You get to decide what happiness is for you. You get to determine your own dreams. You get to set your own goals and limits. Only you know what an ideal life looks like for you. Create your own roadmap for success and follow it.

Gold Mind Work
1. What are you really passionate about?
2. What makes you happy, what are you doing?
3. What do you need to change in your life to be happier?

Gold Mind Mantras
- ◊ I will not place other people's opinions above my own happiness.
- ◊ I deserve to be happy.
- ◊ I wake up happy every day.
- ◊ I will live a healthy, happy life.
- ◊ I am happier than I've ever been.

KNOW YOUR WHY

Your life needs a compass, a guide, to give you daily direction.

Without it, you'll find yourself wandering aimlessly, searching for a destination you can't seem to reach. You'll feel as if you are shooting in the dark, seeking but never finding what really fulfills you. Your purpose, your reason for living, is what drives you and every decision you make. Without purpose, life can be good. But rarely, if ever, will it be great.

If God is at the center of life, which he is in mine, you understand that we all were created to do something specific in this world. It could be to help others, make a difference, or support a cause you believe in.

Whatever it is, your purpose is something that is assigned to you, and something you are uniquely created to do. It's time to discover yours.

When our heads, hearts, and hands are all connected and moving in purpose, it's impossible to remain down in life for long. Purpose-driven people may get knocked down in the pursuit of purpose, but they will always, always get back up. Purpose is a fire inside of you that can't be extinguished. Purpose is your BIG WHY that is your reason for living.

Are you clear on your purpose? If your answer is "no", start by asking yourself a few questions:

- ◊ What do you love to do?
- ◊ What would you do for free?
- ◊ How can you help and serve other people?

Once you've answered these questions, look for the common thread that holds them together. Your answer is your WHY.

Your WHY will keep you up at night and wake you up in the morning, excited to pursue it. For example, my WHY is to motivate people to do what inspires them. I live that purpose out every day. I volunteer at schools. I donate books to daycares. I help friends, family, and coworkers be the best versions of themselves. The joy I receive from helping someone else is a feeling that cannot be replaced. It's priceless.

My why is also for my family, my children, my wife and my future me. I wake up every morning with a laser focus to own my day. I must make sacrifices to put my family and the generation behind me in the best situation to win. My why is to help create content that will help shape a new generation. My why is to leave a footprint along with a road map to success for others. My why is to leave this world better than the way I found it. Go find your why, your purpose, your passion and then help someone else create there's.

Here's the truth—your life is so much bigger than you. Yes, you should want to be successful and live a great life. But a great, fulfilling life is not just about what you do for yourself—it's about what you can do for others too.

Find your purpose, live it out, and watch how much happier you feel.

Gold Mind Work
1. What is your WHY?
2. Who are the people that you desire to serve with your WHY?
3. How can you begin to share your gifts with them today?

Gold Mind Mantras
- I was born to make this world a better place.
- I have so many gifts and so much talent to contribute to this world.

BE YOUR OWN INSPIRATION

We all have someone who inspires us—people we look up to for one reason or another. It could be because of how successful they are, how great they are as a parent, or how confident they are in front of people. There's nothing wrong with that. We need role models and heroes. But here are some questions that I want you to ask yourself:

- ◊ Do you inspire yourself?
- ◊ Are you proud of who you are?
- ◊ Are you your own superhero?

If not, you can change that.

You are more accomplished and successful than you think. I'm sure you never thought of being where you are, doing the things you have done, or meeting the wonderful people you have met. Don't bank your success on what it should look like in other people's eyes because they are not running your race, nor are you running theirs. Don't forget the obstacles you faced to get where you are. Look back and see those footprints of your success.

There is no reason why you can't be the most inspirational person that you know. In the same way that you admire others' strength and how they've overcome so much, give yourself that same credit—if not more. No one knows how much work you put in day in or day out. No one knows what you are really fighting to have what you have or to get where you want to be. You deserve just as much credit as the next person. Don't discount your own determination and strength.

It's also important to remember that everything you see may not be as picture-perfect as it appears. When watching someone from a distance or through the limited lens they offer to the public, we have no idea what challenges or setbacks they've faced. It's easy to see the lights and success, but not the struggle and the sacrifice. We have to be careful to not covet someone's glory without knowing their full story.

But there is one story that you can be certain of, and that's your own.

Your life is a book, and you are the author. Every day, you are writing a chapter filled with lessons that you learn as you grow. Your book's pages are overflowing with inspiration. You are the main character, the star of this story. It doesn't matter who else is watching. You are doing this for *you*. There is nothing more motivating than your own purpose and WHY.

Inspire yourself and be your own superhero.

Gold Mind Work

Think about the goals you want to achieve. For example:
1. What career do you want to have in 1 year? 5 years? 10 years?
2. Where do you want to live?
3. Do you want to have children?
4. Do you want to get married?
5. How much money do you want to make?

Be very specific with your responses. Write down the expiration date of your goals and commit to sticking to the timeline you set.

Also think about the qualities you want to develop, particularly those that will help you reach your goals. For example:

1. Do you need to become more disciplined?
2. Do you need to be more trustworthy?
3. Do you need to improve your confidence?
4. Do you need to become a better public speaker or improve your communication skills?

List the characteristics and habits that you need to become the best and highest version of yourself. Now, think about how it would feel to reach your goals. Do you feel inspired? Why?

Gold Mind Mantras
- ◊ I am the most inspiring person I know.
- ◊ I live a life that I can be proud of.
- ◊ I am capable of creating the habits I need to reach my highest potential.

PART TWO
WHAT YOU DO

PRACTICE SELF-CARE

How do you take care of your mental, physical, and emotional health? Do you make yourself a priority? If not, now is the time to start. You should always be at the top of your priority list.

If you can't care for yourself, how can you care for others? How can you show the people in your life how you should be treated if you aren't treating yourself well? Let me help you: it's impossible.

We are so used to running hard for everyone else that we forget we need time with and for ourselves.

As I am writing this book, we are in the midst of the Covid-19 pandemic, something we've never experienced before.

Almost overnight, we went from living in a world where we could move around freely to work, go to school, and socialize with people we care about to either being completely locked down in our homes or incredibly cautious about where we go and what we do. Covid-19 has changed our social lives and restricted us in ways that many of us never imagined.

For many of us, socializing kept us sane. Without people, we feel lost. But while being separated from people is hard, what this situation has taught us is that we need to find creative ways to stay grounded and happy.

That is true self-care.

Hobbies are a great way to bring some happiness into your life. These activities becomes our go to when we need to condition our minds and refocus on the positive, escape from day-to-day stress, and breathe a little.

What daily activities make you happy? Is it painting, journaling, working out, spending time with family, cooking, or meditating? Is it being social at work? Is it being home, sipping tea, and reading a book? Is it being around friends and family who share the same visions as you or who are inspiring others to do what they love to do?

(Notice I didn't list drinking or any other activity that can affect your health negatively. Your happiness hobbies should be activities that are good and healthy for you.)

Working out is something that I do to take care of myself. I work out about six times a week. Some may say that's too much, but the gym is how I *reset* my day. It's my time where I can zone in and think about lifting those obstacles, chasing my dreams, or pushing past those limitations that were put on me as a troubled youth. I work out for myself, not anyone else. It's enjoyable for me.

I understand everyone's form of self-care may be slightly different, but I challenge you to do something different and see how much joy it brings. We all need a daily "reset" button.

A reset button is a personal empowerment button that helps you refocus on your main goals. I want you to think of something you can do daily to reset.

Identify something that is positive and uplifting that can help you to decompress and mentally energized. It does not have to be one thing, it can be several.

You can read a fictional book, listen to music, go for a walk, or take a peaceful bath.

What have you done for you today?

If you don't have anything now, take some time to figure out what that is. Self-care is the best care.

Gold Mind Work

1. Take out a pen and a sheet of paper. Write down what makes you happy. Don't stop until you've created your full list of happiness.
2. Every day, choose something from this list to do for yourself.

Gold Mind Mantra

- ◊ No matter how hectic my life gets, I will set aside time to do something for myself.

GET CONFIDENT

In basketball, an accurate 3-point shooter is very confident that they can make the shot. They're confident because of their ability. They've practiced this shot to perfection, so whenever they step onto the court, there is no need to question what they can do. There is no need to worry. There is only focus and an inner assurance that the outcome will be positive.

Once you've perfected something—conquered it—you become certain that you can do it again and again. The repetition sends a positive message to your body that you can stand tall, smile, and feel self-assured. Your mind says, *Don't worry. I've got this.*

That is confidence.

Our confidence is built by our accomplishments. Think about that time you set a goal for yourself. It felt good to decide you were going to go after whatever that was, but how did you feel once you reached it? I'm sure you were overjoyed. That feeling you had when you finally got that win boosted your confidence instantly. You knew what it took to get where you wanted to go and you deserved to feel proud of yourself. Once you hit that goal the first time, I bet you were certain you could do it again. The next time you faced that same challenge, you didn't have to spend as much time talking yourself into it. Your fear decreased and your confidence increased. That is the same sense of belief you should carry in everything you do.

How confident are you? Are you certain about the value that you bring and what you do well? Can you enter into a room and demand the attention you deserve or do you try to keep your head down and not be seen?

If you need to increase your self-confidence, here are a few ways that have worked for me:

- ◊ **Be fearless.** Confident people don't doubt themselves. With the mindset that anything is possible, they bet on themselves. They take risks. They aren't jaded by failures, understanding that there are always lessons in losses. So, if there is something that you want, go after it fearlessly.
- ◊ **Monitor your progress.** If you have a big goal to achieve, the journey can be overwhelming and it's easy to feel defeated before you even

get started. But if you break that huge goal into smaller, actionable goals, write them down and track the progress along the way, you'll be able to count a win each time. Every time you reach a smaller goal, imagine how you will feel. That feeling is what builds confidence. Track your wins every step of the way, not just when you reach the finish line.

◊ **Don't worry about what others say or think.** There are so many people in the world and I am sure they won't agree with everything you do, and that's okay. Think about those naysayers who doubted you, those friends and family that didn't believe in you. Let that energy be fuel to push you forward, as opposed to fear that holds you back.

I've applied each of these tips to my life, but there are so many other ways to build confidence. Find the tools that work for you and use them consistently. When it comes to reaching goals, the key is to know how to get your head in the game and stay there. When you believe in yourself and your potential, anything is possible for you.

I DARE YOU to become the person they said you would never be.

I DARE YOU to own the attitude of being comfortable with who you are (but not cocky).

I DARE YOU to bring your charisma, character, and smile into every room you walk into.

I DARE YOU to do everything you set your mind to.

I DARE YOU to be exactly who you were born to be.

Do you accept the challenge? I hope so.

Gold Mind Work
1. What is something you never thought you would achieve but did?
2. Take a huge goal that you have and break it down into smaller goals.
3. Which of those smaller goals have you already reached that you should be proud of?

Gold Mind Mantras
- ◊ I am confident in my skills and abilities.
- ◊ I am confident in who I am and what I can do.

SPEAK NICELY TO YOURSELF

How many times have you heard a parent yelling and saying hurtful things to a child and cringed? You say to yourself, *how could someone possibly speak to a kid or anyone they love, like that?*

Well, that is exactly how you sound whenever you have a bad moment.

When you make a mistake, do you beat yourself up? Do you call yourself stupid? Do you declare that nothing ever works out for you?

Replace that negative self-talk with kinder words. Affirm yourself every day. Just like physical exercise builds your body, speaking kindly and gently to yourself builds your mind.

My favorite affirmations are "I AM" statements. These are powerful declarations about who you are. You can start with these:

- ❖ I AM healthy.
- ❖ I AM strong.
- ❖ I AM beautiful.
- ❖ I AM happy.

When you wake up in the morning, look in the mirror and own the day. Start with a smile, then speak your positive affirmations, and grab hold of that positive attitude. Rebuild your mind and character using words that can make you become who you want to be.

As you begin to affirm yourself, you may not feel that way yet. But keep repeating those words to yourself every day, at least once. Eventually, your mind will catch up and begin to believe it.

I remember hearing a reporter asking the late Michael Jackson, "What comes to mind when you think about music?" His reply? "I AM music." Now *that* is a powerful statement. He completely claimed an entire industry as his own. In his mind (and many of ours too) there was no one greater. With a mindset like that, it was impossible for him to go into a recording studio and fail.

Take a note from the King of Pop and believe that you are the greatest at what you do. Decide who you are and refuse to settle for anything less. Stop beating yourself up and start building yourself up.

Gold Mind Work
1. What is one thing you criticize yourself for?
2. How can you turn that negative into a positive?

Gold Mind Mantra

Complete this sentence:

I AM _____.

WRITE DOWN WHAT YOU ARE GRATEFUL FOR

Thanksgiving shouldn't be the only day of the year when we acknowledge how grateful we are. When was the last time you paused and reflected on things that are often taken for granted? Food, clean water, shelter, family, friends, and access to computers to work and learn, all seem like small things—until we think about the millions of people in the world who don't have them.

In the first part of this book, we talked about starting each day on a positive note by meditating in the mornings about what you are grateful for. Once you have mastered that, take your gratitude practice further and start writing out your gratitude list.

Creating a gratitude list helps you identify the little things that are easy to take for granted, like having a reliable car to get back and forth to work, having health insurance for ourselves and our family, or having three meals every day. These are all precious gifts that so many don't have. And we should be grateful when we are blessed to have them in our lives.

Don't take life, or anything you have, for granted. Each day we get to wake up is a reason to be grateful. Next time you want to feel how blessed you are, just take your hand and place it over your heart. The breath in your body is a gift.

Every night, I write down everything I'm grateful for. It brings me happiness and peace of mind before I go to bed. I encourage you to do the same. Gratitude opens doors to deeper relationships, improves health and self-esteem, and reduces aggression. Collectively, these benefits can lead to a longer life.

Here are some other ways to practice gratitude:

- ❖ When you wake up, and before you reply to texts, emails, phone calls, or messages on social media, reflect on five things you are grateful for. Write them down every morning.
- ❖ Don't forget about the people in your life. What about that close friend who's always there through thick and thin? When was the last time you told them you are grateful for their friendship or took them out for dinner just to say thank you? Thank your loved ones for believing in you, thank your parents for raising

you, and thank your mentors for taking the time to help you identify your strengths.

- ❖ I can't stress this enough—don't forget the small things. We wake up every day but forget to be grateful that we woke up. We can see and hear, while many can't. We eat several times in a day, but we forget that others are starving. I want you to take the time each day to focus on the small things that usually go unnoticed.

Gold Mind Work

Make it a daily habit to write down what and who you're grateful for.

Gold Mind Mantra

Complete this sentence:

I am grateful for
_____.

MAGNIFY YOUR STRENGTHS

What are you good at? What's easy for you that might be hard for others?

Take a moment to reflect on your answers.

You could be a good communicator, a problem solver, an excellent cook, brilliant at tennis or archery, an outstanding barber or beautician. Find something you're good at, identify it, and magnify it.

That's not to say that you should disregard your weaknesses, but you can spend less time dwelling on them. Instead, use that precious time and energy to build on things you're already good at.

It's said that it takes 10,000 hours to become an expert at something; how many hours are you putting into your craft?

Gold Mind Work
1. What are you naturally good at that you could become an expert in?
2. How can you improve? List the books, classes, and mentors that could help you. Create a plan to get access to them.

Gold Mind Mantras

Complete this sentence:

I am exceptional at

_____.

LESSONS NOT LOSSES

How much better would you feel if you looked at life as a series of lessons instead of losses? We have to view adversity differently, or we could head down the road of defeat.

When we don't show up the way we would have liked or we give our all and still miss the mark, something takes over our minds and tries to convince us that we're failures. We can't shake what happened, and we often become hyper-focused on the defeat.

Instead, we should tell ourselves that a setback is just a moment in time. It doesn't define us. And it certainly can't stop us from pursuing our goals—unless we choose to stop there.

There is always a lesson to learn. What did you learn from the class that you scored below average in? You learned that you need to study harder or ask for help. What did you learn when you didn't get the job you always wanted? Maybe this isn't the right time. Perhaps you need to take a deeper look at the company, try to understand their visions, goals, and objectives, and determine how you can align your goals, visions, and aspirations with theirs so your resume and interview will be solid. You might need more development in a certain area. Take a step back to reevaluate how you can come back better and stronger. Don't give up.

I applied several times to become a Chicago police officer when I was 21. It was a dream for me. I went to college and obtained a degree in criminal justice. I became a security guard. I even volunteered at the local police department to surround myself with people in the field. Even with the degree, my experience, and the people I knew, it wasn't enough to become a police officer initially. I must admit, I felt defeated. I was heartbroken, and at such an early age, I didn't know how to take setbacks.

After many attempts, I finally turned that brick wall into a door and walked through it. I'm here to tell you that I would not have become a police officer if I had looked at that obstacle as a failure. I knew the time wasn't right. But I knew one day, it would be. And I would be prepared when my time came.

What if I'd taken no for an answer? What if I hadn't continued following my dreams? If I'd stopped, I would not have the career, and all the opportunities that came with it, today.

As I've gotten older, I've removed the words "failure" and "losses" from my vocabulary. Those words only made me feel defeated. I replaced them with "lessons" and "learned." Even when I make a mistake, I still count the experience as a lesson that I needed to learn, not as a failure or a loss. That perspective energizes me to do better next time.

Here's the truth about mistakes: we all make them. Mistakes are common, inevitable, and *okay*. Take it easy on yourself. It's bad enough to take criticism from others, let alone yourself. Instead of looking at your mistakes as failures, view them as lessons. Make failures and setbacks fun. Embrace your mistakes. Own that mistake and move on. Don't dwell on it. Making mistakes is how we learn and how we can perfect our craft.

I think of life like this—if you're not winning, you're learning. Often, we get depressed, sad, unmotivated, and feel worthless because things don't happen as we want them to. But we should always remember that life is full of twists and turns. All we need to do is learn how to navigate it.

I dare you to take the plunge, go try something new, and fail big at something. Then, sit back and smile and ask yourself, "What did I learn?"

Gold Mind Work
1. What goal are you pursuing right now that has you feeling stuck?
2. How can you turn that brick wall into a door?

Gold Mind Mantras
- ◊ I don't lose. I learn.
- ◊ This may not be the right time but soon it will be *my* time.

TRANSITIONING

You may think of transitions as the journey from childhood to adulthood when we become parents or start a new job. But, in reality, we transition every second of the day, exchanging one state of mind for another.

When we wake up, we transition from being asleep to being awake. When we arrive at work, we go from feeling relaxed to feeling tense. When we get home from work, we stop being an employee and become a mom, a dad, a husband, or a wife. Being aware of your transitions and how you show up confidently, powerfully, and positively in each role will keep you mindful of your environment, help you manage your emotions (for the sake of you and everyone else around you), and make it easier to adjust to new situations. This is mindfulness—intentionally controlling your mind and behavior.

Let's look at an example with a friend, Michael.

By practicing mindfulness, Michael has become great at transitioning. This has helped him in both his personal and professional life. When he gets home from his stressful day as a police officer, he transitions by taking a cold shower, performing a five-minute meditation, and saying the words, "I release any tension I have and I set the intention I want."

This ritual helps Michael transition from being a police officer into a loving father and husband. Although his wife may ask, "How was work?" he is reluctant to tell her because he has a new intention to bring into his home only love, respect, happiness, caring, and positivity.

If Michael were to disclose the fatal accidents, abusive domestics, the homeless youth, and the starving single parents he encountered, he would bring the wrong intention and energy into his home. Michael made a decree never to take work home or take home to work. Instead, he purposely decides how he shows up and what he shares, in every environment. This helps him manage his energy and take control of his "transitions".

You can apply this same practice to your life. Set the intention for who you want to be in every area of your life. Be mindful of the energy that you bring into each space. When you do, you'll find it easier to move through life as a happier person.

Gold Mind Work
1. What are the different roles that you have to transition between in your day-to-day life?
2. How do you need to show up differently in each of those roles?
3. What rituals can you create to help you to transition from one role and mental space to the next?

Gold Mind Mantra
◊ I can transition with control and ease.

GIVING

While it's always good to receive, it's better to give. To have a positive and winning mindset, you have to be a giver. Giving to those less fortunate than us can make us feel good and give us a boost. Giving does the heart and mind good.

If we help others, it can make us happy too. The euphoria a person feels when they give someone advice, resources, food, or money can be exhilarating. Make an effort to help someone every day. If a friend needs a ride to the airport, why don't you offer? If a colleague is having a bad day at the office, invite them to lunch. Text someone who has been influential to you and let them know how much you appreciate them. Give compliments without expecting them in return. These are all small, practical ways to give something to someone that will mean the world to them and give you a sense of fulfillment in the process.

The joy of helping someone you know is rewarding, but helping someone you don't know is another thing entirely. When we think about helping others, our first thought is to give money. And when we don't feel that we have any to give, we decide not do anything. But giving doesn't always have to be monetary. You could give your time by volunteering, you could use your resources to help people in need, or you could donate used goods like clothes and shoes.

Every year, I donate about 100 books and I volunteer at different organizations. I want to become the person I needed growing up. As a youth, I didn't need money, I needed guidance. I needed someone to help me get to my next level. I had questions that needed answers. Since I couldn't find the support I needed, I tried to figure it all out on my own, learning the hard way, and finding myself in trouble often. I don't regret anything I did because I learned from it all.

But what if I'd had that mentor, that special person, or that volunteer that could have saved me from making that wrong decision?

Now, I am committed to being that person for young people. I have a responsibility to ensure that the young men and women coming behind me don't have to experience what I went through. Paying it forward is deeper to me than buying coffee for the person behind me (although that's a great thing). I want to help change generations to come. So, I give back to them any way I can.

Your cause may not be young people, like mine, but there is somebody in this world that needs you. Get your heart in the right place and give more.

Gold Mind Work

1. Identify ways you can give to people you know and those you don't.
2. Commit to helping someone every day.

Gold Mind Mantra

◊ Regardless of how little or how much I have, I always have something to give someone else.

VOLUNTEERING

There is a quote that says, "What you do for yourself you take with you, what you do for others you leave behind."

The time that we give back to improve someone else's life is a part of a legacy and we shouldn't take those opportunities for granted or miss them entirely.

Volunteering is beneficial to the mind and body. It reduces stress and the euphoria we feel from helping someone else is priceless.

When I'm not working as a police officer, I volunteer with teenagers and speak to them about becoming an adult and help them identify their purpose. I resonate with volunteering with teenagers because I saw there was a need to build bridges and relationships with our young people.

Also, nowadays, there is a barrier between the community and the police. But as I always stress to my fellow officers and my teenagers, you cannot spell community without the word "UNITY." We all need each other to make up a community. From the children to the alderman, we are all essential.

Your community needs you too. Support a cause that's bigger than you. Take time out to volunteer at an organization you feel strongly about. Be the light in someone else's life.

Gold Mind Work

1. Think about where you'd like to volunteer.
2. Find some organizations that can benefit from your time.
3. Reach out to them to learn more about current or future volunteer opportunities.
4. Make some time to give some time, even if it's just a few hours a month.

Gold Mind Mantra

◊ I will give my time and resources to serve others.

SMILE MORE

When was the last time you made an effort to smile? Did you know smiles are contagious?

Putting a smile on your face as you enter the office can change your day, and someone else's. You never know who might be depending on your smile, so don't leave it at home.

Smiling improves your mindset and health too. Your smile sends a message to the rest of your body that you're happy, and studies show that dopamine, endorphins, and serotonin are released when you smile.

If I'm having a character-building day where things haven't gone as planned, I take a moment and give a strong smile. No matter how angry or upset you are, your smile will outweigh the negatives.

Guess what else smiling does? It makes you look more attractive. Who doesn't want to look a little more appealing to the eye? Smiling also makes you look more youthful.

Although getting older is inevitable, you can carry your smile with you as you grow older and you'll continue to look younger every time a smile crosses your face.

Smiling and laughter are something we need to do daily. Make it a point to smile more. You'll be happier and so will everyone else around you.

Gold Mind Work

1. Take a moment and smile right now. You just decreased your heart rate and blood pressure.
2. The next time you're out, simply smile and see how many smiles you get back.

Gold Mind Mantra

◊ I always have a reason to smile.

OPEN YOURSELF UP TO HUMOR

Don't take life too seriously. Of course, there's a time and place to be serious, but balance is the key to a positive mental attitude. You need to keep it light sometimes.

As we get older, it becomes uncool to laugh. Some see it as being silly. But it's not.

I'm not saying go around being a comedian all day but look for the humor in things. Everything doesn't have to be tense.

I can remember as a teen, we didn't have to go to the gym to get abs, we just made each other laugh. When was the last time you laughed so hard that your stomach muscles were sore? Find something that makes you laugh that hard again. Trust me, it's good for your body—and your soul.

Did you know laughter is good for our skin, hair, and for fighting off sickness? So, there are health benefits too!

Our daily lives are full of enough stress, so sit back in your seat, put your shoulders back, and get a good laugh in.

Gold Mind Work

Go see a play, stand-up comedy show, or watch a funny movie at home once a week. Do something you love that encourages you to laugh a little.

Gold Mind Mantras
- ◊ My life is full of laughter.

MENTAL HEALTH

We all need a regular mental reset.

Check in with yourself once a week. As a practice to maintain a positive mindset and keep yourself out of those mental ruts, take a moment to think about the lessons you have learned in the past week, reflect on what accomplishments you've made, and determine what you need to work on for the following week.

This will help you stay on course toward your goals and keep you motivated. It's easy to get lost in your day-to-day routines. All too often, our minds can get stuck in "survive" mode instead of "thrive" mode. When you check in with yourself, you can remind yourself that you are moving and progressing. This does wonders for our mental health.

And remember that it's okay not to be okay. When you need to, take time out to speak with someone, especially if you're an essential worker. That's those of you who are doctors, nurses, paramedics, healthcare professionals, first responders, police officers, firefighters, EMTs and teachers. We should check in with one another as well as with ourselves.

Speak with a clinician or someone who can listen. Let them help you work through your mental challenges.

Although physical health is important, mental health is equally as important.

Gold Mind Work
1. Set aside time on your calendar every week to do the weekly check-in above. As a reminder you should:
    - Think about the lessons you have learned in the past week.
    - Reflect on what accomplishments you've made.
    - Determine what you need to work on for the following week.

Write your responses down in a journal or notebook so you can track your progress.

2. Reach out to someone who can be a listening ear for you, if you need it.

Gold Mind Mantra
- ◊ I will prioritize my mental health.

WORRYING

It took years, but I have learned that worrying leads to stress, anxiety, and doesn't do any good.

I've also learned that stress is toxic and can be a bad habit that is hard to kick. When worrying starts to creep in on you, find ways to shut it down and shift your mind back to a positive place.

Our anxiety tends to increase when we lose sight of the present moment. We cannot predict the future and we can't change the past.

So why do we spend so much time worrying about the future and the past, when we can't control them in the first place?

What we can do is handle what is right in front of us. Today's work and responsibilities are enough. If we can take care of those things, while continuing to make progress toward our goals, it's a good day.

Gold Mind Work

1. Be mindful of what you are thinking about throughout the day.

2. Find activities that keep your mind in a positive state. If you can't shake negative thoughts, do something to change your state of mind. Go for a walk, take a shower, or read an interesting book.

Gold Mind Mantra

◊ I will not worry.

STRESS IS AN IDEA

What are you worried about? What makes you feel anxious? What gives you anxiety?

Although we all deal with stress differently, it is safe to say we have all been there before.

There is always a reason to be stressed. Sometimes it's running late to work, not being able to sleep because of a presentation we have to give the next day, or our company is downsizing and we could lose our jobs.

Even good things, like planning for a trip to Paris, can be stressful.

Stress comes from the uncertainty of the unknown. It's natural. But it doesn't have to paralyze us. Noticing stress and managing it from its onset will facilitate a healthier life.

Think about it, most of the time we stress ourselves out because of the possibilities. We ask ourselves, *what if this happens?* as we think through every worst-case scenario possible.

But what if nothing happens besides your blood pressure going up? Is it possible you'll be okay and whatever you are stressed about will work out in your favor? Is it possible that even if something goes wrong, you'll survive? Of course, it is!

You don't have to accept stress as your default. Life can only stress you out if you allow it. It's all in your mind.

Gold Mind Work

When you feel stressed, take a deep breath in to the count of three. Exhale to the count of three. Repeat as needed until you feel your heart rate come down and stress leaving your body.

Gold Mind Mantras

- ◊ I will not allow stress to overtake me.
- ◊ I choose to be stress-free.

MANAGE YOUR STRESS

Believe it or not, it's possible to keep your stress in check. Here are a few tips to help when you feel stress arising:

- Repeat, "I am calm," over and over until your emotions come down.
- Exhale stress by pretending it's your birthday and you're blowing out your candles. Repeat the exhales until you feel calmer.
- Think about the time you were the happiest. Close your eyes and go back to that moment. Stay there in your mind for a while.
- Purchase some lavender spray. When those anxious feelings arise, use that spray to fight off the stress. Inhale the scent to relax your mind and body.
- Carry a stress ball to squeeze when you feel tense.
- Repeat these words until you calm down, "If I can't flea it, don't fight it. Just flow with it." (This is my personal favorite, courtesy of Pastor Joel Osteen.)

If you can't control the problem, why try to fight it? Just let it go and flow with it. Use these techniques to regain control of your emotions, lower your anxiety, and relax as best you can.

Gold Mind Work

Create your go-to kit of tools to help you when you need to bring yourself down.

Gold Mind Mantra

◊ If I can't flea it, don't fight it. Just flow with it.

THERAPY

We've all been through tough times. It could be the loss of a job, losing a family member or friend, failing at something, or experiencing the breakdown of a relationship.

Often, we carry baggage through our lives without even realizing it. Before we can start to grow, we have to heal our open wounds.

Therapy can start the healing process. Eventually, though you'll never forget, you'll get to a point where you're comfortable talking about the difficult things you've experienced.

What's more, your story could help heal others and it could give someone else the push they need to seek help.

If you've never been to therapy, now is a good time to start.

Gold Mind Work

1. Do some research to find a therapist. You can work through your employee benefits, if you

have them, research online, or ask someone you know and trust for a referral.

2. Follow through and make an appointment for your first session.

Gold Mind Mantras

◊ I am worth the investment in my mental health.

◊ It is safe for me to allow someone to help me to heal.

MEDITATION

How do you clear your mind? What's your go-to strategy when you're overwhelmed or under pressure? Is it alcohol, pain relievers, gambling, cigarettes, or marijuana?

There's no right or wrong way to release tension, but some ways are better (and healthier) than others. Instead of turning to those things that have a negative effect on your health, why not try something that can calm you down without damaging your body, like meditating?

Hear me out.

When it comes to mental health, meditation has a lot of benefits. It calms the mind and body. It forces you to be quiet, reflect, and gather your thoughts. By channeling your energy into a more positive state, you'll feel more in control of what is happening around you.

Every morning, I meditate before beginning my daily activities. Since starting the practice, I've noticed that I'm less likely to feel stressed in difficult situations, and I'm more relaxed and aware of my attitude.

Meditation doesn't have to be hard or take a lot of time. To start, just relax, close your eyes, and practice deep breathing—in through your nose, out through your mouth. Repeat the process until your mind is relaxed.

Be consistent and watch how meditation transforms your mind.

Gold Mind Work

Commit to a daily meditation practice. Set aside at least five to ten minutes a day to get still.

Gold Mind Mantra

◊ My mind and body are calm and relaxed.

PICTURE MEMORY

Another powerful tool for positive thinking and mental health is developing a picture memory.

Close your eyes and think about a moment you wished would never end.

Was it your wedding day? Your graduation? A trip to an exotic island? Or was it time spent with a loved one?

Whatever it might be, try to take a photograph of it in your mind, and commit it to memory.

This is a great way to have a mental escape. This can be done at home, at work, or in your car. Close your eyes and think of a place that makes you smile. It's your happy space. If you're not there in person, take your mind to that place. Who is there with you? What does it smell like? What do you see? What do you hear? How does it make you feel being there? Your objective here is to create a calm and peaceful image in your mind.

Having an image in your memory helps you go back to that peaceful place without using your phone or physically being in that special moment.

When things take a turn for the worse or aren't playing out how you expected, you can always close your eyes and go back to that happy place.

Gold Mind Work

1. Make a mental list of your most favorite moments.
2. Practice your picture memory skill the next time you feel stressed.

Gold Mind Mantra

◊ I can always go back to my peaceful place.

JOURNALING

Journaling is good for relieving stress and putting things in the past where they belong. Journals can help clear your head, share your private thoughts, and work through your emotions on your own. You never have to share your journal with anyone. It can be your special place that no one knows about. But if you decide to share your story, I promise you there is someone in the world who needs to hear it.

My first book, *Shadow of the Past*, came directly from my journal. Throughout my life, I have been faced with obstacles and challenges that have helped me build my character. I used to reflect on those dark times, and they kept me up at night. Thank God for my beautiful wife, Patricia. She told me to start journaling to release some of those feelings. Two weeks later, I had a story that would change many lives.

I never knew how my past affected me as an adult, but since I wrote that book my mind has been free. I have been happy, and I have helped others overcome their darkest moments. You never know who could benefit from your story. We all have a unique story that somebody else needs to hear.

Starting a journal is simple. Get a blank notebook (or a special journal if you want something fancy). Write down your positive thoughts, and then write down your negative thoughts. Keep this up for 21 days. By the last day, your positive list should, hopefully, outweigh your negative.

By jotting down your thoughts, you can see, right in front of you, all the negative thoughts bringing you down. As time goes on, and you keep up with your journaling, you'll see that you become more conscious of your thought patterns and, hopefully, realize that you have the power to choose the positive.

Go back through your journal from time to time, and you'll be inspired by how much you've grown and overcome.

Gold Mind Work

1. Purchase a journal.
2. Choose a time of day, ideally in the mornings or before bed, to write.

3. Try to journal for at least 10-15 minutes a day.

Gold Mind Mantra

◊ I will create space in my life to write out my thoughts, feelings, and ideas.

BE MINDFUL, NOT A MIND FULL

When was the last time you went for a walk, got outside, and experienced nature? Walking is an easy way to relax, relieve stress, and clear your mind.

Take 30 minutes out of your busy week and try it. I want you to leave work, negativity, the past, bills, or anything else that can jeopardize your peace behind.

While you are on this walk, observe the colors you see, listen to the wind blow, hear the birds chirping, and take deep breaths. Really breathe in the air. I want you to regain your inner peace, so be careful not to bring any distractions along with you.

As you are walking, be mindful of how you are feeling and your posture. Ensure you are walking upright (shoulders back, chest out, and with a big smile). Be mindful of the things around you and take this moment to just relax.

Often, we think we are relaxing just because we are physically away from children, work, and chores. But we have to distance ourselves mentally too.

It's not very relaxing, even if you are in a relaxing location, when you have a full mind, thinking about what you need to do tomorrow, what bills you have to pay, what person made you mad, or what you're having for dinner tonight.

Just be in the moment to relax and find your happiness.

Gold Mind Work

Schedule some time to take a least one 30-minute mindfulness walk per week.

Gold Mind Mantra

- ◊ I will set aside time to improve my mental and physical health.

EXERCISE

There's no saying truer than "Your health is your wealth."

Exercising 3-4 times a week is a great way to stay healthy, but once is better than never.

It doesn't have to be a workout at the gym, either! Daily walks, taking the stairs, parking at the end of the parking lot; it all helps.

When you're at work, get up from your desk every hour, stretch, and walk around. Making these small changes will allow you to live a longer, healthier life.

Gold Mind Work

If you don't schedule the time to exercise (or do anything for that matter), it's less likely to happen. Put the days/time that you will exercise on your schedule and stick to it.

Gold Mind Mantras
- ◊ My body is healthy.
- ◊ Exercise is a necessary investment in my health.

PRACTICE WELLNESS TO PREVENT ILLNESS

Moving your body is only one piece of your wellness puzzle. What you eat and how much you rest are important too. When you exercise and eat healthier, you'll find that the quality of your sleep will improve as well.

I'm no nutritionist, but I make healthy choices by following my 80/20 rule. My 80/20 rule consists of eating healthy 80% and having my fun foods the other 20% of the time. I must say, I am a fan of a good slice of pizza, but the key is not having too much.

Having a healthy diet plays an important role in the sleep you get. Once your health is in order, you will have a better quality of sleep. Some may think that they have gotten rest because they had 8 hours of sleep, but that isn't always the case. Your objective is to have a better quality of sleep, not a higher quantity. You can have a good night's rest with 6 hours of sleep, or you can wake up tired after 10 hours.

When it comes to your health, think about how you can be proactive instead of reactive. If we take care of our health, it can prevent us from many illnesses, doctor's visits, and medications. Good health saves us time and money.

You have a lot to accomplish in this life, and you need a healthy body to get there.

Make your health a priority.

Gold Mind Work

1. Commit to reducing unhealthy foods from your diet.
2. Focus on the benefits of a healthier diet. How will you feel if you are able to eat healthier?
3. Notice improvements in your health and sleep.

Gold Mind Mantras

◊ I will make healthier choices for my body.

◊ Food is my fuel.

◊ My body is healthy and will carry me through everything I need to do.

WHAT ARE YOU WATCHING ON TV?

Television can have a huge impact on our attitude and perspective on life. Let's take the news for instance. Watching sports, weather, and traffic is okay, but the top stories of murders, attacks, and other horrifying events can have a negative effect on how we feel.

When you first wake up in the morning, your mind is most vulnerable and open to anything and everything. How can you have a positive and productive day if your mind has just been exposed to the 'deadliest weekend this year' or some other negative news?

As soon as you hear something like that, your mind is subconsciously stricken with fear. Now your morale is low, you have negative thoughts racing through your mind, and you become cynical and jaded.

Watching negative news reports is never a good idea, but if you decide to tune in, do it in small doses. Guarding your mind is essential to having a positive attitude and an optimistic day, so keep watching the news to a minimum.

Gold Mind Work

Avoid news in the morning. Do your gratitude, journaling, and meditation first. Then, scan the news if you need to.

Gold Mind Mantra

- ◊ Everything around me is positive. I don't need to be afraid.

WHAT ARE YOU LISTENING TO?

It isn't just what you watch that can ruin your positivity—what and who you listen to can also have a negative effect on your mood.

Take music for instance. I choose to listen to jazz and classical music because both genres allow me to feel at ease and retain a sense of peace. That type of music helps me to stay calm and be mindful of my attitude and actions.

On the other hand, there are types of music that can put your mind in an aggressive state. For example, if you're driving to work and your listening to screamo music to, it could influence you to drive faster and more recklessly, meaning you're not vigilant of other vehicles, pedestrians, and traffic laws.

In addition to music, podcasts are a great way to develop and grow. Through the host's experiences, you get to see life or business from a different point of view.

Think of an area you would like to improve in. It could include positive thinking, how to become healthier, or how to grow your wealth, for example. Use your smartphone to turn your car into a university, rather than a club. Whenever you're driving, instead of blasting your favorite song, listen to a podcast. I guarantee you'll learn something new.

Think about the hours you spend in your car or commuting and imagine how much you could learn in a week, a month, or a year.

Use the free time you have to make yourself better. Make every minute count, and don't just count the minutes of your day.

It may seem like a small thing, but it's really not. Your ears and eyes are the gateways to your mind, so you have to be careful about what you hear and see.

Gold Mind Work

1. What types of music do you listen to most? Does it put you in a positive, confident frame of mind or a negative frame of mind?

2. Change the music you listen to so your mind is filled with more positivity than negativity?

3. Pick at least one topic that you would like to know more about. Then research podcasts on

that topic. Try at least one new podcast a week.

Gold Mind Mantra

◊ I am guarding my mind by listening to music that uplifts, calms, and encourages me.

◊ I am constantly expanding my mind.

WHO ARE YOU FOLLOWING?

Social media is a platform to conduct business, meet like-minded people, stay in touch with family and friends, have fun, and much more. It is a great tool, depending on the user.

But social media can also have a negative impact on you as well. Some use it to commit crimes, taunt, and harass others. When spending time on any social media platform, be careful.

When you look at who you are following and interacting with online, be sure those media outlets and the people you are connected to through social media have similar visions to yours.

Social media should be a fun, useful tool to improve your life. If it's not doing that for you, change how you use it!

Don't let social media interrupt your mindset.

Gold Mind Work

1. Go through your social media accounts and unfollow anyone who is causing you to have a negative mindset or is not aligned with your vision.

2. Find 2-3 accounts to follow that inspire and help you to reach your specific goals (financially, physically, etc.).

3. Try to limit your time on social media, and don't compare yourself to others.

Gold Mind Mantra

◊ I use social media as a tool to build myself up, not tear myself down.

◊ I do not need to compare myself to others.

INVEST IN YOURSELF

We must invest in the most valuable tool we have, which is our mind. Every day, we must do something that stretches us. If it makes you uncomfortable, you are doing it right. Doing what is easy will keep you in a fixed mindset.

We can't always depend on what's familiar because what is familiar will keep us stuck.

What are you doing to develop yourself personally? Are you reading a book about a subject you're unfamiliar with? Are you learning a new language? Are you taking up a new trade? Are you taking that course in school that you've always been afraid of? Have you used that gym membership that you purchased at the beginning of the year? Have you consulted with the doctor and the nutritionist to see what routes you need to take to a healthier lifestyle?

If you feel called out on all the things that you promised yourself that you would do, but haven't, it's okay. Give yourself grace.

But get to it! It's nothing but fear holding you back from trying something that you haven't done before.

Go for it. What's the worst that could happen?

Gold Mind Work
1. Pick one area of your life that you are afraid to make a change in.
2. What is the change you'd like to make?
3. Why are you afraid to tackle it?
4. Who can help you overcome your fear?
5. What BIG goal can you set related to that change?
6. Break your BIG goal into smaller goals. Set deadlines for each.
7. Start working on your plan.

Gold Mind Mantra
- ◊ I can do things that I've never done before.
- ◊ I am constantly stretching myself.
- ◊ I am willing to step outside of my comfort zone.

SETTING GOALS

There are three different types of goals: short-term, intermediate, and long-term. Short-term goals take less than three months to achieve, intermediate goals take between 3 and 12 months to achieve, and long-term goals take more than 12 months to achieve.

Throughout life, we may often have all three types of goals set for ourselves at one time. But don't let that overwhelm you! Don't be afraid to set goals. Goals are your guide toward greatness. Without them, you won't know where you are going or how to get there.

You could have financial goals, relationship goals, professional goals, and personal goals. Here are some additional categories of goals that I recommend having, especially if you are unsure about where to start with goal setting:

Spiritual Goals: These are important. When people hear "spiritual", their first inclination is often to think of religion. Although religion plays a role, when I say spiritual, I'm talking about self-love and making yourself happy. Establishing goals to feed your spirit in some way will help you establish the right foundational mindset to achieve everything else you want in life.

Health Goals: Did you start exercising, but stopped when you didn't see the results you wanted? Your health is your wealth. If you haven't been able to consistently make your health a priority, setting some specific goals in this area may help.

Financial Goals: Are you living paycheck to paycheck? Is your money spent before you receive your wages? If so, setting some financial goals will help you tremendously. Why not work on putting together a budget to streamline your finances and ensure you're never left in a difficult financial position? It's useful to have an emergency fund that is around three times your monthly expenses, and preferably six times your monthly income. Make it a goal to focus on your money.

Relationship Goals: How healthy are your relationships with friends, family, and your significant other? Your partner might have different goals and views than you, which isn't a bad thing, but you need to know if you are both headed in the same direction. You cannot have a sustainable relationship if one person loves to shop, gamble, and take trips, and the other wants financial independence, to create wealth, and invest. The same goes for your friendships. Some friends are leeches and can suck us dry. We listen to their problems and run to them when they have an emergency, but when it's time to reciprocate, we get nothing but excuses. Any relationship is about give and take, not just take. Create a relationship goal to have healthier, mutually beneficial relationships so you can cut out the parasites.

Career Goals: Are you in the position you want to be in, or are you settling with what was given to you? Perhaps you need a goal to move from where you are now into a new career. You don't have to stay in the same industry or continue with the same type of work. You can choose whatever field or position you think you will thrive in.

If you want to move into a new industry, it's a good idea to do your research. Your big goal is to make a career move. Set some smaller goals to speak to someone just starting in the position, someone who has been there for over 5 years, and someone who has been there for over 20 years. Having these discussions with the "boots on the ground" people can help you make a wiser decision.

Once you've identified your goals, make sure to write them down somewhere and monitor your progress. The joy you will feel once you have accomplished your goals, when you get to cross them off, will be truly wonderful.

And don't stop there. Once you achieve one goal, start working toward a new one. Always have something to chase.

Gold Mind Work

1. Choose your goals. Make them BIG enough to scare you but not stop you.
2. Write them down with timelines and deadlines.
3. Get to work!
4. Monitor your progress.

Gold Mind Mantra

◊ I will achieve my goals.

TAKE ALL THE STEPS

I know we are all in a hurry to get to the next level, but each step is important.

I didn't realize this until I became an adult. I was racing up the stairs of life trying to get to the next level. Suddenly, I missed a step and fell flat on my face.

Instead of trying to skip steps and race up to get to the top, I learned that every step matters.

You have to be patient and take life (and your goals) one step at a time. In life, we like to use the elevator or escalator because it gets us to the next level more quickly, but we have to be mindful that if we get to the next level and we are not prepared, then the blessing becomes a burden.

Each step we take toward our destiny is preparing us for our next level.

Gold Mind Work
1. What goals are you rushing toward and making mistakes along the way?

Gold Mind Mantra
- ◊ I may be moving slow, but I am moving.

PLAN FOR OBSTACLES

As the old saying goes, "Anything that can happen will happen."

We all know it's true, and that's why it's best to have a backup plan. For every one of your goals, you should have a Plan A *and* a Plan B to get there. So, when one door closes, or you hit a dead end, you can change course and keep going.

For example, if you've applied for another position at work, but you weren't chosen, don't feel too disheartened. Instead, look at it as a chance to improve for next time. It'll give you more time to plan and prepare for the next opportunity that comes your way.

While you're waiting for your next opportunity, get prepared. If you had a Plan B, get to work on that. In the job example above, maybe your Plan B is to speak to someone in the department to get a heads up the next time the position is available or find out what you can do to stand out. Depending on the situation, your Plan B may be to apply at a different company.

The point is, don't stop!

Doors get closed. Things go wrong. A delay is not denial. It's a sign to look for another path.

Your next opportunity is around the corner. How prepared are you?

Gold Mind Work
1. Look at your list of goals.
2. For each one, figure out what your Plan A and Plan B will be to reach them.

Gold Mind Mantra

◊ I may have to slow down, but I won't stop.

◊ I have many paths to reach my goals.

CHALLENGES

We've all faced challenges, and we know we'll face more in the future. It's when we face challenges that we're allowed to evolve. Think of challenges as opportunities for future success.

I know you've heard the saying, "If it were easy, everyone would do it." Your goals aren't easy. You need tenacity and strength to see them through. This is why being challenged is so important. Challenges prepare you to fight for your future and prove that you are willing to do whatever it takes to get to where you want to go.

If you were an employer and you had two applicants with the same degree, same age, and same experience, but one faced a lot of challenges and the other didn't, who would your top pick be? The struggles they've been through to get to their current position is proof they won't be phased by future challenges. Challenges shape our character. Take every challenge head-on.

Let me share a challenge I am dealing with now. At the time I am writing this book, we are dealing with a global pandemic (COVID-19). I've had an uncontrollable cough for weeks and couldn't get rid of it. I took the coronavirus test and tested positive. I felt defeated and devastated once I received those results. I had friends and family who passed away from this virus, my wife is pregnant with our second son, and our 15-month-old son is at home.

I immediately thought, *how can I tell my wife that I have tested positive*? I knew she'd be terrified and afraid of what the outcome would be. She was pregnant, and the stress I would put on her would be enormous. Before I talked to her, I took a deep breath, mediated, and prayed. I mustered up enough courage to tell my wife the daunting news. Thankfully, she was supportive and positive. However, I knew we had to discuss isolation. Being separated from my family while I was quarantined would be so hard for us.

I had no problem wearing a mask outside, but wearing a mask in my own home was very challenging. I had to use separate washrooms from my wife. I couldn't kiss, touch, hug or lay next to her. I'm used to eating dinner with my wife, but for two weeks we had to eat separately. I couldn't help her take care of my son so she could get the break her pregnant body needed. I couldn't see my oldest son at all. It was even worse that I could hear my family playing and I couldn't do anything besides talk to them through video chat. For two weeks, I couldn't go outside or see anyone. You would have thought this virus got the best of me, but it didn't.

I refused to let Covid-19 beat me down. I kept my mindset positive, determined that I was going to come out on the other side of it. And I gained much more than I lost. The bond my wife and I created being physically apart made our marriage deeper. Having this away time from everyone allowed me to slow down and listen to my heartbeat, listen to my thoughts, and be grateful that I am still here. I would rather go 14 days without seeing them than go a lifetime.

After my 14-day quarantine, I was able to embrace my family and remember how much it meant to be able to touch and hug them. My love for my wife and children was stronger than ever. I stay in gratitude for my family, but even I needed a reminder of how much they meant to me and to never take them for granted. My sickness may have seemed like a challenge (which it was), but it was also a precious gift.

No matter what challenges you face, don't look at what's happening *to* you. Look at what's happening *for* you.

Gold Mind Work
1. What challenges are you facing right now?
2. What positives can you take away from them?

Gold Mind Mantras
◊ There are gifts in every challenge that I face.
◊ I am stronger than I know.

REWARD FOR SUCCESS

Celebrate the small wins. Every step toward your goals and aspirations is a success. You could celebrate by going out to a nice restaurant, going on a scenic walk, taking yourself on vacation, seeing a movie, or even by exercising. You must celebrate those small wins to keep you going.

No matter how small a step toward your goal is, when you take it, you have to celebrate it. How many times have you said you wanted to start a new fitness routine or live a healthier lifestyle? A small win could be buying your comfortable workout shoes and a nice workout fit. What about that glass of wine you have every day? You scaled back to every other day. Celebrate those small beginnings because they can lead to big wins!

Gold Mind Work

1. Think about your goals and write down all your wins, big and small.
2. Congratulate yourself and celebrate! You deserve it!

Gold Mind Mantra

◊   I am worthy of celebrating all my wins.

ORDINARY MOMENTS

We often go through life looking for those "home runs", those extraordinary moments.

But have you thought about the ordinary moments that can be just as special?

If your mom calls you every day to say hello, don't take that for granted. If you have a parent or grandparent who talks too much, cherish it because, one day, you will yearn to hear their voice again.

Being positive means cherishing the ordinary moments most people take for granted.

Gold Mind Work

1. What is something that seems small that makes you feel special?

Gold Mind Mantra

◊ My life is filled with special moments and special people.

TAKE IT AT A GRADUAL PACE

What are you doing right now to help you move toward your goals? Even if you are taking baby steps toward your goals, progress is good.

Be careful not to confuse complaining about something with progress though.

Complaining pushes, you further away from your goals. The energy you use to complain could be put into taking steps toward your goals.

Take time to enjoy the journey; each step toward your goal is a success.

Gold Mind Work

1. When you talk about your goals, are you complaining that you are moving too slow or praising yourself for moving at all?

Gold Mind Mantra

◊ Every step I take is progress.

PROCRASTINATION

Don't put things off for another day when you can do them today.

It's funny, we don't procrastinate to do something easy like watching Netflix, having a drink, or hanging with friends and family. But we make so many excuses to avoid the hard things like working out, cleaning, or finishing an assignment. I was told once that how you do anything is how you do everything. And it's true.

Think about it, the way you do one thing shows up in every part of your life. If you're spending most of your off-time watching TV, scrolling on social media, or lounging on the couch, chances are you are the same way when it comes to your relationships, health, and work.

Les Brown said it best, "If you do what is easy, your life will be hard. But if you do what is hard, your life will be easy." Don't shy away from what's hard. Doing what is hard today will make your life so much easier tomorrow.

Own your day and make every minute count. Avoid procrastinating by creating a daily, weekly, and monthly to-do list. Having a to-do list is very important to keep you focused, on task, and accountable. It will feel like your worst enemy, but a to-do list is really your best friend.

You must be able to trust yourself with keeping your word to yourself and getting things done. You cannot expect people to trust and believe in you if you don't believe in you and honor your word.

Gold Mind Work
1. What areas or tasks are you procrastinating in/on?
2. Make a to-list that includes those things.
3. Stick to it! Don't allow yourself to make excuses. Sacrifice socializing and fun to get it done.

Gold Mind Mantra
◊ I will keep my word to myself by doing what I promised myself I would do.

COMMUNICATION

How are your communication skills? Are you able to understand and be understood by others? How well are you at listening, speaking, observing, and empathizing? These are all important skills to have.

As a great communicator, you'll feel more confident whenever you have to present in front of people or facilitate a conversation of some sort. Even in your personal life, people appreciate someone who listens well and makes them feel validated and heard.

Communication isn't just face-to-face interaction or over-the-phone conversations. It's also digital like social media, emails, and other electronic communications. We can all become great communicators.

Here are some tips to improve your communication skills:

Active listening: Active listening is very important in communication, and listening is just as important as speaking and writing to express yourself. When listening to someone talk, are you tuned in to them or are you distracted by your cell phone or laptop? An active listener is present, attentive to, and engaged with the person or people in the room.

Ability to convey ideas: To become a great communicator, you must be able to present a problem and give solutions and ideas to help resolve it. This is how people see you as a leader and someone worth listening to. A good communicator must be clear about what they are trying to convey. If you're speaking in a small room, you must be able to adjust your voice so everyone can hear and understand you. Being too loud in a small room could come off as yelling or disrespectful. Be able to adjust your tone and voice for the audience in front of you.

Receiving feedback: How are you at giving and receiving feedback? A great communicator must be able to convey feedback in a way that that is helpful and not harmful. At the same time, you should be able to receive feedback and use it to improve.

Be aware of non-verbal cues: Non-verbal communication is important too. Take a comedian for example. They have to learn how to monitor the audience to see if they have their attention. Once they have your attention, they spend a little more time on the topic to keep everyone engaged. But if the audience is having side conversations, on the phone, yawning, and not in tune, the comedian changes the subject to capture their attention again.

The same approach applies to you. Great communicators know how to read a room. You must watch for non-verbal cues like your audience's body language, facial expressions, and eye contact. This will let you know if you are interesting to the person or just wasting your time.

Be sure to brush up on your communication skills. Whether in your professional or personal life, great communication skills will take you far.

Gold Mind Work

1. On a scale of 1-10, how great are you at verbal communication?
2. On a scale of 1-10, how great are you at listening?
3. On a scale of 1-10, how great are you at non-verbal communication, like writing or interacting in digital spaces?

For the areas where you scored lower than you'd like, how can you improve your communication skills?

Gold Mind Mantra

◊ I am an excellent communicator.

SOCIAL ATTUNEMENT

We live in a social world, whether it's through social media or being social with others in person.

But often, when we are socializing, we are not in tune with the people around us. Is it because we love talking about our victories or our problems? Is it because we love when people listen to us because it makes us feel important? Or is it because we fail to care about anyone else but ourselves?

Whatever the case may be, let's be more mindful of others around us. Let's have more social attunement skills.

Social attunement is a very underutilized skill but it can be learned. Developing this skill will help you be more dialed in and connected with other people's feelings and thoughts.

Having this skill will help facilitate deeper connections and deeper relationships. Because being fully aware and tuning in to someone else lets them know you really care about them.

Next time you are having a conversation with someone, give them your full attention, ask questions, and be involved not just present.

Gold Mind Work

The next time you are interacting with someone, put your phone or anything else that can distract you away, and be present in the conversation. Repeat this practice until it becomes a habit.

Gold Mind Mantra

- ◊ When I am with people, I make them feel valued, seen, and heard.

WATCH YOUR WORDS

Words are very powerful. They can help you or harm you, and that goes for what you say about someone else as well as what you say about yourself.

Think of it like this: you say to yourself *I'm fat, I'm ugly, I'm stupid.* Referring to yourself like this will have a negative effect on the rest of your life. You internalize that criticism, and, over time, you believe it. Once you have children, you could pass down your negativity to them, and the negativity will continue.

No matter what, your words should put you and the people around you in an inspired and positive state of mind. We don't realize that once we choose to use negative or derogatory words when talking about others, we are actually cursing ourselves.

For instance, John decides to disrespect Jim. In turn, Jim disrespects John. Jim has vowed he will never talk to John again because he felt disrespected. Not only has John created a war between him and Jim, but he has also lost a friend.

No matter how angry you are, you must be mindful of the words you use. Remember, once words leave your mouth, you can't take them back.

Keep negativity out of your mind so that you don't hurt yourself. And keep negativity out of your mouth so you don't hurt anyone else.

Gold Mind Work

When you are angry, don't rush to speak negatively to yourself or someone else. Calm down and clear your mind. Never speak out of anger.

Gold Mind Mantra

- ◊ I have complete control over the words I say to myself and others.

WHAT SUCCESS LOOKS LIKE

What does success look like for you? Is it that big, beautiful house with the dog, white fence, roundabout driveway, two cars, two kids, a beautiful wife, or a handsome husband?

Or is success simply living out your purpose in life?

Maybe you want it all. You get to decide. Your only job is to define success for yourself and be constantly moving in that direction.

I once heard someone say, "If you were on trial for being successful, would the judge and jury find you guilty?"

If the answer is "no", you have some more work to do.

Start trying to understand your meaning of success and work out how you're going to achieve it. Success is subjective, what does it mean to you and no one else.

Gold Mind Work

1. What is your vision of success? Write it out and include all the details.

Gold Mind Mantra

◊ My vision of success is my own. I get to choose what success means to me.

VISUALIZE SUCCESS

Go to a quiet place, close your eyes, and think about what you want out of life.

Think about how you'll know when you have it. How will you feel? What will your life look like?

It's important to be clear about what the realization of success looks like so that when it happens, you don't miss it because you are so focused on getting to the next goal.

If you are hesitant to allow your mind to visualize success, you are facing fear.

Your dreams may be so big that, from where you're at now, they feel out of reach. But remember, if you can just visualize and focus on the small steps toward success, they'll take you to where you want to go.

Sometimes your goals are so big they scare you, which can be great because it keeps you striving for something. But your goals should challenge you, not scare you.

If you feel that a goal is too big to conquer, break it into some smaller steps that will take you in the right direction. Your success will be so much easier to see and visualize.

Gold Mind Work

1. What is the next goal that is right in front of you?

2. Does it feel scary to you?

3. How can you break that scary goal down even further into smaller steps that feel more realistic for you?

Gold Mind Mantra

◊ My goals are within reach.

ACCOMPLISHMENTS

Before bed each night, write down seven things you want to accomplish the next day. No matter how small the task is, write it down. For example:

1. Make someone smile.
2. Read 10 pages of a book.
3. Go to the gym.
4. Eat something healthy.
5. Help someone.
6. Make a list of things I'm grateful for.
7. Cook a new dish.

Remember how we talked about the value of a to-do list? This is an example of that.

Not only does a list like this keep you on track, but it also helps you manage your time. The main thing you want to accomplish with this exercise is learning how to have control over your life and your day.

The feeling of satisfaction you get when you check everything off your list will help you maintain a positive mindset. Nothing pumps you up more than accomplishment! It's the fuel you need to keep moving forward.

Gold Mind Work

If you have not adopted the habit of making your to-do list each day, start today.

Gold Mind Mantras

- ◊ I have enough time and energy to get through everything I need to do today.
- ◊ I have control over my time and my day.

MOTIVATION

What is your motivation? What do you enjoy doing that brings you self-gratification? Is it reading, working out, helping others, drawing, or singing? Whatever the activity is, make sure it's for your personal reward or self-gratification.

Oftentimes, we only do things because we want to be rewarded for it, whether it's for money, gifts, or just applause. As human beings, we yearn for that support from strangers because we may lack that component from the people, we care about most.

I can remember being in high school and not having that support or validation from my father. This led me to seek support from anyone else I could find it from. These influences might have been negative, but that was the attention I was looking for. I was doing things just to be accepted and praised by people. I felt that any support was better than none. I needed other people to motivate and accept me. Now, I know how to do that for myself.

Learn how to self-satisfy and not look for extrinsic motivation. You can be your own supporter.

Think about what drives you. What comes to mind? Money, fame, material goods, social status, luxuries? These are the rewards a person could receive when they are driven by extrinsic motivation.

We are all guilty of this. If we have a job, we work and then we get paid. When we work hard, we get more money. When we do a great job, we're rewarded with incentives. This is normal, but it shouldn't be the only reason why you do something.

Read a book because the storyline sounds interesting and you want to know what happens, not because you have to do a book report. Learn to play an instrument to be a more well-rounded, interesting person or to have a creative outlet.

Find something that brings you happiness and self-satisfaction. Your mind will reward you for it.

Gold Mind Work

When was the last time that you did something simply because you enjoyed it?

Gold Mind Mantra

- ◊ I am putting my happiness first.

DO IT FOR MORE THAN MONEY

If your primary motivation is always money, I want to encourage you to rethink your mindset.

Money is a tool that can bring you freedom, opportunities, and options, but it can't make you happy.

Many millionaires and billionaires have had a lot of money but weren't happy throughout their lives. But there are many people who make less than $50,000 a year and are beyond happy.

Which life would you rather have?

There's nothing wrong with pursuing materialistic things, but it could become a problem when it's your sole motivator.

Money comes and goes, but time, health, and relationships are what sustain you. These are the things that truly make you happy.

You want a meaningful life, with or without a lot of money. Make happiness your priority.

Gold Mind Work

1. Are you chasing money or happiness?

Gold Mind Mantra

◊ Money is not the sole focus of my life.
◊ I am chasing happiness not money.

EQ VS. IQ

Our emotional intelligence, or EQ, dictates how we show up in our relationships.

People with a high EQ tend to be more self-aware, level-headed, are very good at communicating their emotions, and understanding others. A high intellect (IQ) can get you far in life by being smart. A high EQ can arguably get you further by being sensitive to people in the world around you.

If you are wondering how high your EQ is, here are some questions to ask yourself:

- Are you good at controlling your emotions?
- Are you aware of when you are feeling angry, happy, or sad?
- Do you handle your anger well?
- Are your relationships smooth?
- Are you a good communicator and listener?
- Are you flexible and adaptable when things are out of your control?
- Do you hold yourself accountable or do you blame others?
- How honest are you with yourself?

- Are you trustworthy?
- Are you assertive and confident?
- Are you decisive?

If you answered "no" to most or all of these questions, then you are probably lacking in EQ.

Developing a high EQ is not easy but it can be done through being aware, reading books, coaching, and learning more about yourself.

Gold Mind Work

1. Do some research on books and trainings on EQ. Commit to learning more tools and techniques to help you.
2. Put what you learn into practice at work and in your relationships.
3. Look for improvement. Do you feel more confident? Are you more in control of your emotions? Are you less angry and frustrated? These are all indicators that you are growing in your EQ.

Gold Mind Mantra

◊ I am working on my EQ and becoming a better version of myself.

INTELLECT vs. INSTINCT

Many of us go to school to gain intellect, but we forget about the importance of our innate instinct. These two go hand in hand.

In school, we get an education on subjects that interest us or may help us pursue different careers. And while that kind of "book knowledge" is incredibly beneficial, when you are meant to do something in life, you will also have an instinct and natural drive to be successful at it. It's the kind of desire that can't be learned from any book. When that kind of instinct takes over, you refuse to give up until you're doing what you were created to do. You feel out of place doing anything else. These are the truths that a classroom can't teach you.

No matter how many degrees we earn, no matter how many letters we have behind our name, no matter how many titles we hold, if you don't have the instinct to pursue your purpose, your time in school was just a passing of time. We must use our intellect along with our instinct to fulfill our purpose.

As babies, when we are unable to communicate our problems to our caregiver, our instinct is to cry, pout, or throw a tantrum. However, as adults when we face obstacles, setbacks, or problems, we must not use our instinct as we did when we were babies. We must focus on our end goal and do what is necessary to get us closer to our purpose. Our instinct gives us the ability to be resilient, adapt, and become who we need to be to get us to that next level.

A bird's instinct is to fly, a fish's instinct is to swim, a lion's instinct is to hunt.

What is your instinct? What were you created to naturally do?

Gold Mind Work

1. What subjects or topics are you interested in learning more about?
2. What do you do naturally well?

Gold Mind Mantra

Complete this sentence:

I am made to _____.

MONEY MANAGEMENT

Having money is important, but controlling your money is essential. It is almost impossible to stay in a positive frame of mind when your money is a mess. The feeling of living paycheck to paycheck or drowning in debt could lead to depression. If you can control your money, you can control your life and have the resources to invest in your future.

Here's how I gained control of my life and my money:

- I saved at least 10% of my take-home pay.
- I started spending less.
- I paid off debt.
- I started investing.

The first goal is to control where your money is going, set a budget, and watch where you spend your money. By knowing your expenses and your net income, you can quickly identify how much disposable income you have.

I know most people hate the word "budget", because it might make them feel restrictive or like they can't spend money. So, let's call it "cashflow". Cashflow is taking the time every month to identify where your money goes. Step one of money management is to understand your cashflow.

Every month, create a spreadsheet with separate columns for income, expenses, and total. Populate the columns. This will give you insight into how much you have coming in and going out so you can plan more, have more, and invest more. As you get more control over your spending, you can easily identify what makes you happy. Are you buying something because you really need it or is it a waste?

It's also important to understand what's an asset and what's a liability. As Robert Kiyosaki stated, "Assets put money in your pocket and liabilities take money out." While liabilities are inevitable for most of us, strive to spend more money on assets than liabilities. For example, having an income property is an asset. Every month you are paid by your tenant to occupy your property. On the other hand, a liability is a brand-new car. It's an asset for the bank, but a liability to you.

Ideally, you want to leverage your assets to cover your liabilities. You can purchase an investment property that brings in enough money to cover your car note. This is a great financial strategy and shows how you leverage your finances in a smart way.

Money management may seem overwhelming at first, but believe me, you can do this. See this as an opportunity to sow seeds into your success. With more money, you can elevate your life and reach your goals faster.

You have the power to control your future right in your pocket or purse. Use it.

Gold Mind Work

Set aside time to create your monthly spreadsheet and track your expenses.

Gold Mind Mantras

- ◊ I will control my money.
- ◊ When I manage my money well, I am investing in my future.

PLAY THE OFFENSE

As humans, we tend to wait until a problem arises to pay attention to it. This is particularly true when it comes to our money.

Things like retirement, savings, and paying expensive tuition for ourselves or our children are all big goals and problems that we'd rather not tackle. So, we tuck them away in the back of our minds until we're forced to deal with them. Sometimes we get a chance to tackle them before it's too late. That's if we're lucky. Our futures come at us fast. And then small problems become big headaches that we have to scramble to handle.

Many people wait until it's too late to start investing or get a handle on their finances. I was one of them. I waited until my car needed fixing before I saved money to fix it. I used my savings account as a checking account and buying a pair of sneakers was my emergency.

After being caught out there in the deep end enough times without a life raft, I learned how to manage my money better and save for those rainy days. It wasn't easy at first, but I knew that emergencies were a lot more stressful and harder to handle when I didn't prepare.

I want you to be more financially savvy than I was. Start today. Have an emergency fund. You never know what might happen, and it can never hurt to be prepared.

Gold Mind Work

1. What was the last financial emergency you had?
2. Were you prepared to handle it?
3. How can you adjust your expenses to save that amount, so you are prepared if there is a "next time"?

Gold Mind Mantra

◊ I am financially prepared for whatever comes my way.

LEARN WHAT YOU CAN CONTROL

In life, there are some things we can control and a lot that we can't.

We can't control the traffic. We can't control other people or how they feel about us. We can't control our past.

But what we can control is our perspective on the things that happen to us and how we respond.

The next time you feel the urge to get frustrated about situations that come up for you, take a step back and think about whether or not you have any control over it.

If not, is it worth wasting energy on? I hope you see that the answer is no.

Gold Mind Work

Look at any challenges you are currently facing and frustrated about. Is there anything that is out of your control? If so, commit to taking it off your mind.

Gold Mind Mantra

- ◊ I am focused on the things in my life that I can control.

SET ALARMS ON YOUR PHONE

So many of us have these beautiful and expensive smartphones. Let's look at how we can make them work for us.

We have alerts, reminders, and timers on our phones to remind us to wake up, work out, study, go to a meeting, be somewhere important, but we never set a reminder to keep us positive and happy.

For example, I have several reminders set at various times throughout the day. The reminders are titled "BRING THE JOY."

When that notification goes off and I am feeling anxious, angry, or unmotivated, it helps me get back on track. I might have had a disagreement with someone or feel defeated because of work, but my reminder pulls me back to the reality of being positive. It is a great way to own your day.

Set a reminder for yourself every 2 to 3 hours. The title of the reminder should bring you joy, peace, and happiness as soon as you look at your phone.

Gold Mind Work

Create your positivity reminders. When they pop up on your phone at the designated times, don't ignore them, even if you're busy. Take the time to reset your mind.

Gold Mind Mantra

- ◊ I can bring joy, peace, and happiness into my mind and heart whenever I need to.

CHECK YOUR POSTURE

Having good posture leads to confidence. Be very conscious about the way you walk, sit, and stand. Believe it or not, you are signaling to the people around you that you're not confident if your posture is not good!

In addition, having good posture reduces lower back and neck pain. Most importantly, having great posture makes you happier and more energetic.

Let's take a moment to check your posture. What does your posture say about you? If it's nothing positive, let's change that. Are your shoulders back and chest out? Are you standing tall or are you hunched over, with your head low?

When standing, keep your feet shoulder-width apart, keep your head level, tighten your stomach, keep your shoulders back and make sure your weight is on the balls of your feet.

While walking, tighten your stomach, keep your chin up, avoid leaning backward or forward. Stand tall.

If you are sitting down, keep your feet flat on the floor or on a footrest, and try to avoid crossing your legs.

Make sure your back is against the chair and your knees are at the same height or lower than your hips.

Lastly, avoid sitting for more than 30 minutes at a time. Take a break and go for a walk or do some stretching.

Gold Mind Work

Do a posture check throughout the day. Adjust your body when you are standing, walking, or sitting.

Gold Mind Mantra

◊ I am confident at all times.

DECLUTTER YOUR LIFE

Let's look inside your personal space. When you enter your home, office, or room, do you feel happy or stressed?

If you feel happy, this is a great sign that you are utilizing your space correctly. However, if you feel stressed and frustrated, now is probably the time to declutter.

Do you have piles of mail, old paperwork, and bills? Consider getting file storage, so that all your paperwork or bills can be put in order.

Are loads of laundry and clothes all over the place? We are all guilty of having a pile of clothes on the bathroom, bedroom, and closet floor. Having a laundry basket in the rooms where you change clothes could be helpful.

Are old pictures, antiques, or just random stuff sitting around? Again, we are all guilty of collecting stuff. But the question is, do you really need it? If a burglar broke into your home and took it, would you be mad? Would it even matter? When decluttering, this is what

I want you to think about: If I never saw this item again, would I care?

If the answer is "no", sell it, donate it, give it away, recycle it, or trash it.

Use this same strategy to declutter your home or your office. The rule of thumb is: If you buy a pair of shoes, a pair of shoes should be donated, bartered, or sold. If you buy a new pair of slacks, you must throw out a pair of slacks.

Our rooms, homes, and offices are cluttered because we add but never subtract. We must get rid of those things we don't wear or use.

A clean, clear space equals a clean, clear mind.

Gold Mind Work
It's time to clear space. Take one room at a time, and work through the decluttering strategy. Get rid of items you no longer need. Find storage space and items to neatly store what you need and use.

Gold Mind Mantra

◊ My spaces are clear. My mind is clear.

MAJOR VS. MINOR

Your time is more important and precious than money, so watch how you spend your time.

your time could be stolen by pondering over minor things, like being cut off by someone who is in a hurry, or by spending time on social media going back and forth with someone who doesn't support your views.

You could be wasting your time talking with friends and family who don't get your vision.

These things are minor and should be avoided at all costs. If you use so much energy on the minor things, you won't have any left for the major things.

Ask yourself whether this will matter five minutes, five months, or five years from now?

If the answer is "no", let it go.

Gold Mind Work

1. What are you regularly wasting time on that you need to eliminate from your life?

Gold Mind Mantra

- ◊ My time is precious, and I will only use it on things and people who matter to me.

TAKING THINGS PERSONALLY

You must not take things personally, because this is a recipe for disaster. Taking everything personally means that you are always mad at something or someone because of what they said or did. Remember it's not you, it's them.

When we don't take things personally, we accept the fact that everyone has their own opinion, and that is what makes us individuals. Not taking things personally also gives us the power to control our emotions and our attitudes. Just because someone doesn't like your views, it doesn't have to be the end of the world. Just move on. Place yourself in that person's shoes. If they didn't have the exact same upbringing as you, how can they understand your point of view?

Think about that time someone called you a nasty name. How did you feel? I'm sure you were angry and hurt to say the least. It stuck with you. But if you can think about it in hindsight, does that person know you? Are they projecting their anger, envy, or insecurities onto you? I know it's hard to think that way in the moment. But it's a skill you must master if you want to keep your mindset and perspective in a positive place.

I must be transparent and admit that I am still a work in progress in this area. As police officers, many times we are degraded by unruly citizens. However, as a professional, I must keep my game face on, no matter how hard it is. If I took every negative response personally, I couldn't remain in the positive headspace I need to be in to do my job well. The same goes for you.

When you take things personally, you lose control of your emotions, so remember: this is only one person's opinion. There are many more opinions out there, and I'm sure you don't have the time and energy to give your power to someone else. Put that energy toward something you can control.

And let me add this: don't allow even the *positive* opinions of others to affect you too deeply. Do you get excited by compliments to a point that you can't live without them? What about that feeling you got when your crush gave you a compliment on social media? How did you feel then? Happy, excited, confident, on top of the world?

Placing your trust in what others say is a huge no-no. Learn to feel that way about yourself without the need for validation from others. It's not that you shouldn't accept compliments, but you shouldn't take compliments or comments personally because it can drive your emotions too much. Self-esteem (emphasis on *self*) is important. Your esteem should be based on how you feel about yourself, not how others see you.

Gold Mind Work

> 1. When you catch yourself getting offended by someone's opinion, breathe through it. Smile. Move on.
>
> 2. Use positive feedback for your own good. Take all those great compliments you have received over time and write them down and put them in a box, keep them in your journal, or put them in your phone. Whenever you feel down and need a confidence boost, take another look at them.

Gold Mind Mantra

> ◊ I don't allow other people's opinions to affect me.

TAKE THE HIGH ROAD

We are often faced with situations that could make us lose our cool, or react in a way that's belittling or disrespectful. I once learned there were three "roads" of how you could treat people.

Let's start with the low road. Along this road, you treat people worse than they treat you. For example, you're in traffic and another vehicle cuts you off. The person looks at you and apologizes, but you flip them the finger, honk the horn, and curse them out.

In the same scenario, taking the middle road is when you treat people exactly how they treat you. Taking the middle road, you would still react to the person who cut you off, but you would be aware enough to see that the driver was apologizing. You can catch your emotions and be able to control your reaction.

Taking the high road simply means treating people better than they treat you. In the same example, a person cuts you off, but you gave them no reaction or emotion. You ignore their actions and don't give them further thought. Taking the high road should be the standard we strive for.

We never know another person's situation. In this example, the person who cut you off might be in a rush to get to the hospital to spend the last moments she has left with her mother. Given this information, would you allow her to cut in front of you? I'm certain your answer would be yes. This is why taking the high road is so important, because we never know what someone else is going through.

Gold Mind Work

1. How often do you find yourself taking the low or middle road?
2. How do you feel after those interactions?

Gold Mind Mantra

◊ I always take the high road.

SEPARATE YOUR FEELINGS FROM YOUR PERFORMANCE

I understand life isn't fair, and you deserve more than what you have. You've been working hard, doing the right things, and it feels like you should have it all. But you must separate your feelings from how you perform. Your breakthrough is around the corner. So, you can't quit now, even if you want to.

Although I have never run a marathon, I can imagine the hardest part is the last few miles. Those are the times when you push through the pain, the mental block that's telling you to quit, the blisters on your feet, and the sweat running in your eyes. Everything in you wants to stop because it's so hard. But if you can just hang in there for a few more feet, you can cross that finish line, put the pain behind you, and celebrate your win.

You must continue to show up as the best version of yourself no matter how hard it is. I can remember working in an environment that was very challenging. I felt as if I was a target for what I believed in. Depending on your job, each one has different cultures, and this one was no different. It was hard to navigate the politics, attitudes, and negative environment.

However, I did not allow the job or the environment become who I was. Every day I had to mask my thoughts, feelings, and emotions. I was the first one there and the last one to leave. I went above and beyond my scope of work. Even though my efforts often went unnoticed, I never let how I felt jeopardize my character.

Eventually, I moved on and up to another, more rewarding position. And there was nothing negative that my supervisor or co-workers could say about me. Someone is always watching to see if and when you slip up. I never gave anyone that opportunity. I knew I'd done my best.

It's okay to bend but don't break. Don't allow a negative situation that you may be in to cause you to lose sight of your goals or your character.

Your win is coming.

Gold Mind Work

1. What tough situation are you feeling tempted to walk away from out of frustration?

2. How can you adjust your mindset to tough it out?

3. What are the benefits of staying and doing the best you can? What will you learn? How will you be better?

Gold Mind Mantra

◊ I can do this.

CYNICISM

When you smell flowers, are you thinking of a funeral or a beautiful garden? When you look out the window, do you see the stain on the glass or a beautiful day? If you always see the negative in things, you might be a cynical person.

I can remember being that kind of person at the beginning of my career. I worked nights, and I slept most of the time with blackout drapes to keep the sun and the world out.

I hated being around people, so I avoided large crowds. I enjoyed being home alone or with people who understood me, so my circle was small. I saw everything negatively. Thankfully, my wife came along and changed my life for the better.

She noticed these things and was brave enough to tell me I needed to seek help for this reality I was creating. At first, I thought she didn't understand the things police officers face on a daily basis, but I took a deeper and closer look at myself and realized she was right.

Everything I said or did was negative. I told jokes that were negative, my comments were negative, and I had nothing positive or inspiring to say. Although I didn't seek outside help from counselors or therapists, my wife and I were able to work through this difficult time. I was able to save my relationship and my life.

If you are a cynical person and someone has tried to talk to you about your attitude, listen. Sometimes we don't realize that we've become jaded, and we need someone else to point it out to us. Once it's bought to your attention, be committed to changing. You'll be better for yourself and for them too.

Gold Mind Work
1. On a scale of 1-10, how cynical are you?
2. If you answered 5 or above, how has your negative perspective affected your life and relationships?
3. If you were to change, how do you think your life and relationships would improve?
4. Are you willing to change?
5. If so, choose one thought you can change from positive to negative. Then, choose one relationship where you can do the same.

Commit to a shift in both. Observe how much better you feel. Use that motivation to continue to work on other areas and relationships in your life.

Gold Mind Mantras

- ◊ I am a positive person.
- ◊ I see life positively.
- ◊ I see people positively.

IT'S OKAY TO SAY NO

We all have that friend or family member we cannot resist hanging out with.

But you must ask yourself a few questions before committing. Is this in my budget? Does this person add to my life, or subtract from it? Is our conversation healthy? Can we talk about the present, not just the past?

Saying "no" isn't a bad thing, it just means you are very intentional with your time.

Evaluate the value of your relationships. Sometimes our long-term relationships are the most toxic, whether it's a friendship or a significant other.

Just because you've known someone for a long time, it doesn't mean they have your best interests at heart. Those toxic relationships could be holding you back from meeting people who can add value to your life.

Gold Mind Work

1. What relationships in your life have reached their expiration date?

Gold Mind Mantra

◊ I only have room in my life for people who add value to it.

CHOOSE JOY

We have all done something or worked somewhere that didn't make us happy.

Most of the time, we are pressured by our peers or by the salary a job offers.

When was the last time you chose joy? We never know when our time is up, so why not choose happiness?

You can make more money, you can meet new people, but you can't make more time. Do whatever brings you joy, whatever wakes you up before the alarm clock, whatever you would do for free.

What can you do now that your future self will thank you for? Sometimes winning isn't about landing that job or coming in first place.

"Winning" could be taking the first courageous step and being bold enough to not allow fear to keep you confined.

Gold Mind Work

1. What in your life is not bringing you joy?

2. How can you begin to move away from those things and into more happiness?

Gold Mind Mantra

◊ I am choosing joy.

BELIEVE IN YOURSELF

I once heard that many people believe in ghosts more than they believe in themselves. That resonated with me because it is true. Don't stop dreaming.

I like to go to sleep thinking of my dreams, so I can wake up with goals to conquer my dreams.

Why not write down what you dream of every night? I am a huge fan of writing things down. It will motivate you to wake up with a purpose.

Before I started writing down my dreams, I woke up with no drive or motivation. I had no vision, no purpose, and no understanding.

I hung out with people who didn't fit into my destiny, I dated women who weren't aligned with my purpose, and I made decisions that could have cost me my goals.

But I never lost sight of my dreams or stopped believing in myself. Having my dream notebook saved my life and my destiny.

Write your dreams down. Believe in them and yourself.

Gold Mind Work

Get a notebook and write down your dreams. Commit to writing something every night.

Gold Mind Mantra
- ◊ I believe in my dreams.

HUMAN BEING NOT HUMAN DOING

Most of the time, we want to give everyone the best version of ourselves, but we fail to give *ourselves* the best version of ourselves.

If we are no good to ourselves, how can we be any good to anyone else?

Think of life as a glass of water. Each day we have a full glass. Throughout the day, we pour a little here, a little there, watering someone else's seed.

At the end of the day, we might be thirsty or need our seed watered but we have nothing left.

It's okay to just *be*.

What does that look like?

Being mindful of everything. Being at one with yourself. Being at peace with what's going on in the here and now.

Gold Mind Work

Create some space in your day or week to just be. You may be unable to travel somewhere to be alone, but you can take a walk or find a quiet space in your home. Wherever you are, allow yourself the time and space to refocus on your now.

Gold Mind Mantra

- ◊ I am good to myself, so I can be good to others.
- ◊ I am at one with myself.

ENJOY THE PROCESS

Be patient during the process and enjoy the journey of becoming.

We live in an era of instant gratification.

This is why the fast-food industry is booming. We go through the drive-thru and get an entire meal in less than five minutes. We want to drive in the fast lane because we don't want to sit in traffic. We want to throw things in the microwave instead of cooking. We want to get hired and become the CEO by the end of the month. We want to catch the elevator instead of the stairs. We want those quick weight loss solutions instead of doing the workouts.

We may get those quick results, but often, we struggle to sustain them because we aren't prepared.

It takes time to get to the top. And remember, a blessing given too soon can be a burden. Enjoy the process so once you get there, you are better prepared.

Gold Mind Work

1. Where are you feeling pressured to press through your process?

Gold Mind Mantras

◊ I am not rushing anything.
◊ I am trusting my process.

GET UNCOMFORTABLE

I must be honest, I never enjoyed reading. Any opportunity I had to push away a book, I did. I did not enjoy homework, schoolwork, or any other paperwork. I was very comfortable with not reading because I didn't think it would benefit me much. Fast forward to now, and my favorite hobby is reading. I am so disappointed that I missed so much knowledge over time.

From becoming a reader to an author, I have noticed a dramatic change in my vocabulary, my perspective on life, and my communication. I had to get past the feeling of being uncomfortable until reading became comfortable for me.

In life, we do what is easy because it takes little to no effort, but it's actually killing us in the long run. Today, I want you to identify something you have been putting off. Working out, going back to school, learning another language, purchasing that house, investing in real estate or stocks, applying for that position at work. Whatever it is, just go for it.

If we don't stretch, we can't grow and we begin to have a limited mindset.

This is more important if we have someone who looks up to us. Our protégé sees us as their mentor. If we have a limited mindset and don't fulfill our goals and aspirations, how can we tell someone else to fulfill theirs? We should lead by example and step out of our own comfort zones to see what possibilities are waiting for us.

Remember this quote: "Whatever you are not changing you are choosing."

Gold Mind Work

What hard things are you avoiding in your life?

Gold Mind Mantra

◊ I am willing to be uncomfortable and stretch myself.

EXPOSURE

A lack of exposure could keep your mind enclosed. Exposing yourself to different things can broaden your knowledge.

What are some things that interest you? What culture is interesting? What food do they eat? What are their rituals and why? Is there a sport you see yourself playing or watching and you'd like to know more about? These are only a few questions I want you to ask yourself. Begin to pique your interest in people, places, and things outside of your current environment. Follow your curiosities to see where they lead.

We enjoy sticking to our culture and family traditions, but sometimes this keeps us limited and mentally enclosed. I was a person who loved to stick to my ways until I met my loving and outgoing wife. She is very adventurous and loves to learn and try new things. To say the least, to remain in her good graces, I had to come out of my shell.

Doing that has exposed me to so much, including learning a second language. I have tried archery and found out it's a very fun sport. I have tried new dishes from other cultures and I have done things I said I will never do again, like zip-lining.

Expose yourself to more than what your environment shows you. Meet new friends, go to new places, and learn how others live. Try new foods and play new sports. These new experiences will help you grow not only yourself but your relationships and connections as well. Experiences like these will also create memories that will last a lifetime. Die with memories, don't live with dreams.

Learning is not only knowledge; it is exposure. What if you found a new hobby by trying something new? What if you found a new friend? What if you found your spouse by trying this new thing? What if?

What will you lose from trying something new? I'll answer that for you, nothing! But what could you gain? Everything. The things we don't know keep us trapped in a small mindset.

Gold Mind Work

1. Pick one new culture, place, sport, or hobby you've been curious about.

2. Study more about it online.
3. Find something locally that you can do to expand your exposure, like a class, restaurant, or museum. If you can, plan a trip to visit that country or to practice the hobby.

Gold Mind Mantra

◊ I will learn and live fully by exposing myself to new people and places.

NO MORE ZERO DAYS

Wake up every day and do something that can put you closer to your goals.

If it's getting in shape, do one push up, take the stairs instead of the elevator, park in the rear of the parking lot (not that close parking spot by the entrance), or choose a healthy snack once a day.

If it's to learn another language, take 10 minutes out of your day and practice reading and writing the language. If it's to start a business, surround yourself with people in that field or business. Meet up with them for tea, coffee, or Zoom calls. This can be an opportunity to dive in deeper about how to run a business and determine if entrepreneurship is right for you.

This is what I am saying: Do not let a day go by without doing something to get you closer to your goals.

You must take massive action to reach your optimal potential.

Gold Mind Work

1. Did you do something today that was a step toward your goal?
2. What was it?

Gold Mind Mantra

◊ I don't have zero days. Every day I do something productive to lead me to my goals.

NEXT LEVEL

What's your next level? What is the next thing you want to accomplish in life? Everyone has a next level.

In grade school, our next level is high school. In high school, our next level is college. After college, our next level is securing a job that can support us and help pay off those student loans. Once we secure that job, our next level is to move up in that company. Once the promotion comes, the next level could be finding someone to settle down with. Once our spouse comes along, the next level may be having kids.

As you can see, this can go on until our Creator calls us home. For most of us, there is always the next level to reach.

Everyone's next level is different, but you should always work on identifying your next level and how to get there.

There is no right or wrong when it comes to your next level. Remember, this is *your* next level. You may not want kids, and your next level might be to find someone to travel the world with. You may not want to attend college, and your next level might be to go into the professional world straight from school. You might have identified your passion, purpose, or gifts at an early age and your next level might be to find a career or start a business that allows you to use what you were created to do. Maybe you've managed your money well and saved and now you want to start investing.

There are so many opportunities to explore but you have to identify where you are and where you want to go.

Gold Mind Work

Think about what your next level looks like.

1. Are your current goals aligned or do you need to adjust?

Gold Mind Mantra

◊ I am ready for my next level.

ROUTINE

Not to get too biblical, but the Bible speaks about "the little foxes that spoil the vines." That statement refers to those small things we do over time that can either build our character or break our character.

What are those small habits you have that are hurting you? What are those secret habits you dare to tell anyone about? No matter how small those things are, they have the potential to harm us in the long run.

For example, Daniel works at a supply warehouse. He takes home office supplies almost every night. Although it's a small act and it's only pens, paper, or a stapler, over time, he is building a character of a thief. Once he is comfortable taking those small items, his behavior may spiral into bigger items. Before you know it, Daniel has found himself in serious trouble with an employer for theft or, even worse, the law.

This same philosophy works in the reverse too.

Take Patricia for example. She has a habit of working out before work and getting to her job early. This little routine has been going on for five years. She is noticed by her peers and supervisors. Because she has built a habit of being committed and dependable, she was offered a supervisor role. Healthy routines will yield a good return.

Remember, how you do anything is how you do everything. Build that strong character by the good things you do. Good character shows up in everything.

Gold Mind Work

1. What habits do you have that you know are holding you back from being your best self?

Write them out. Be intentional about changing your behavior. It will be hard at first, but it's well worth it.

Gold Mind Mantras

- ◊ I am an honest person.
- ◊ My character speaks positively about who I am.

MIND YOUR OWN BUSINESS

You might have been told before to "stay in your own lane" or to "mind your own business."

In the next section of this book, we're going to talk a lot about people and who you need around you to win. So, this isn't a book about moving through your life alone. But there will always be a time when you need to focus on your own race and your own life.

You should rarely, if ever, be more focused on someone else's life than you are on your own, especially if you're comparing yourself to others.

If we use our life energy toward our goals, visions, and aspirations, we won't have time to cross over into other people's lanes.

I once heard a story about a man who wasn't minding his own business. He went for a jog one morning and, while he was running at his usual pace, he heard footsteps coming behind him. His ego wouldn't allow him to let the other runner pass him, so he took off running faster. After a few blocks, he noticed he was running by himself, and he had passed his home.

How many times are we running someone else's race and missing our own finish lines? We should remember that being unique is what makes us special, so we don't need to compare ourselves or overly focus on what someone else is doing.

Gary Vaynerchuk once said, "Your goals don't have to be big, they just have to be yours."

Are you minding your own goals?

Gold Mind Work

1. How many times a day are you comparing yourself to or competing with someone else?

Gold Mind Mantra

◊ I am running my own race.

ENCOURAGE, DON'T CRITICIZE

Nowadays people judge others on all sorts of things, from the color of their hair to the color of their skin.

Before you critique someone, think about something positive you can say instead.

You may not agree with the way they live their life, and you may not support the things they believe in, but who are you to judge?

Make this part of your daily routine: find someone to encourage and support. Find someone or something to love, not someone to hate. Find the beauty in things and people, not the ugly. Bring the happiness out of people, not the sadness. Look for ways to be a blessing, not a curse.

Don't use criticism to boost your self-esteem or to fit in. In this process, not only are you creating an enemy, but you are also hurting someone's feelings.

Let's build meaningful and sustainable relationships, rather than criticizing and judging someone by the chapter we walked in on.

Gold Mind Work

This is one of the exercises that will force you to check your heart.

1. Are you judgmental and critical? Be honest with yourself. If so, now is the time to change.

Gold Mind Mantra

◊ I see the beauty and good in everyone and everything.

TAKE INVENTORY

Take out a pen, then ask yourself two questions:

1. What have I accomplished and should be proud of?
2. What haven't I achieved that I said I was going to do?

This is your goal inventory. Once you celebrate yourself for your accomplishments, you should also see where you need to focus as you move forward.

Every year, take stock of where you are and where you want to go. Make a list of these goals and attach a deadline to them.

More importantly, surround yourself with people who can help you achieve your goals. Next to your list of goals, write down a few names of people who have experience in the area you need to know more about. Reach out to them and offer coffee, tea, or a lunch and learn date. Be clear and let them know what your goal is. Don't be secretive about asking them for help. Be honest and bold about where you want to go and how they can play a role in your journey.

Gold Mind Work

1. Take your goal inventory.
2. Make your goal list with deadlines and identifying who can help you.
3. Reach out to each of those people and set up some time to ask for their support.

Gold Mind Mantra

◊ I am connecting with the right people who will help me to achieve my goals and fulfill my purpose.

PART THREE
YOUR GOLD CIRCLE

STAYING PRESENT

How often do you check your social media? Is it a distraction that keeps you from socializing with friends, family, and co-workers?

We are social beings and we thrive off of human interaction and socialization. Life is about balance, and this includes balancing the time you spend on social media.

When you are out with family and friends, why not leave your phone in the car and be mentally present, not just physically present? Life is very short and we don't want to waste our precious moments scrolling through someone else's lifestyle feed. Enjoy the company you have around you.

Think about that feeling when it's time to come together, whether it be birthday celebrations, Thanksgiving, or Christmas. Think of that euphoria you feel being surrounded by loving and caring people.

We cannot get that feeling from social media, even if we might think we can. Short-lived joy from getting lots of likes and comments is not the same as the time and connection from people you know and love.

I want to help you focus on the people around you and the people who support you.

To put it bluntly: if you were to die today, how many of your social media followers would show up at your funeral? Think about it.

Gold Mind Work

Try to limit the amount of time you spend on social media. Invest that time in your family and friends in person.

Gold Mind Mantra

- ◊ I am always present with the people I am in the room with.

NO CRYING ALONE

Sometimes crying is a good way to release the pressure you have built up. It's tempting to run and hide when we need to cry. But that's not always healthy.

Crying alone can lead to isolation and depression, which only makes whatever we are already dealing with worse.

When life hits you hard, it's okay to let it out, wipe your tears, and keep going.

Remember how you felt the last time you cried alone. Were you sad, lonely, helpless, and vulnerable? Imagine how you would have felt if you had someone there with you to hold your hand or to hold you? They wouldn't have had to say a word. But you would have had a moment when you felt supported for a change (we all need that).

Identify someone you can be vulnerable with—someone you know, like, and trust. When you need to cry, call that person. Allow them to be your support system and be the same for them.

Your breakthrough could be on the other side of your last tear, so cry when you need to.

But here's the catch: Your pity party should only last 24 hours.

You don't want to drag this on to another day. Release it and get back to your grind.

Gold Mind Work

Find a person who can be your shoulder to cry on and who you can reciprocate that support for when needed.

Gold Mind Mantra

- ◊ I am not weak for crying. There is strength in my tears.

NOT ME, BUT ME TOO

To deepen relationships with others, we must discover and focus on our similarities rather than our differences. It goes back to the saying, "Birds of a feather flock together." What connects us always brings us closer together.

In our conversations, we must magnify our strengths and not our differences.

How often have you been in a conversation that was going well until you disagreed with that person on a subject or a belief? That conversation was an opportunity to learn more about each other and deepen a connection, but, because both of you shut down, that opportunity was lost. In this world, we are so quick to judge or share our opinion with others. But what if we looked for ways to connect rather than separate?

As humans, it's very important for us to not only feel important but feel like we belong.

In conversations, look for ways you can say "me too" rather than "not me." If it's a subject, topic, or belief you don't like or are unfamiliar with, you don't have to disagree or comment. This can be a great opportunity to say "teach me" or "help me understand. "

Saying these two simple phrases can deepen your conversation and relationship with others. This could also help you to be more memorable.

Most of us are so accustomed to meeting and conversing with people who aren't interested in understanding our point of view, especially if it differs from theirs.

When you are open to understanding others and actively seeking ways to determine where you are more alike than different, people will want to spend more time with you and open up more about themselves. Not only will you learn more about someone you didn't know (or do know), you will become a better connector and communicator. Who knows where that could lead?

From now on, focus on what you have in common with others, not what you don't.

Gold Mind Work

The next time you meet someone you don't know well, instead of automatically dismissing them because of your differences, make a sincere effort to get to know them better and find some common ground.

Gold Mind Mantra

◊ I am always meeting someone I can learn from.

SURROUND YOURSELF WITH POSITIVE PEOPLE

You are the sum total of the people you spend time with. Look at your crowd.

Are they helping you reach your potential? Are they fanning your flames or putting out your fire? Are your conversations largely positive or negative? Do they leave you feeling happy and inspired, or feeling sad and down?

Our time is limited, and we don't know our expiration date. But we should be able to live a happy and healthy life, and not let others rob us of our happiness. That is what happens when we spend a lot of time around people who aren't positive and aren't actively working to use and live up to their potential.

I know a lot of people live and swear by Drake's song "No New Friends." But if you've had your same circle for five-plus years, no one has evolved, and you guys are doing the same thing that you did five years ago, there is a problem. Those people are keeping you stagnant. It's time for new energy from new people who can help you get to your next level.

When you think about your friends, ask yourself some simple questions:

- Do they have the same (or similar) goals?
- Do they want the best for you?
- Are they dependable?
- How are your energy levels when you are around them? (Hint: If your energy level is low, you might need to look for a more high-energy group.)

As you think through your responses to these questions, how do you feel? Is your instinct saying that you need new people in your life? You may not need to cut out everyone you know, but perhaps you need to step up and encourage your friends to grow and expand their mindsets. Try something different like meeting new people and then introduce your old group to your new group and have a bigger alliance. We are human pollinators. This is how we form a bigger and more sustainable network.

Always remember: people love doing business with people they know, like, and trust. Become that positive influence energy for others, so you can help create other positive people you can depend on to bring your energy levels up. It's a win for everyone.

Gold Mind Work

Take inventory of your current friend circle. If you are not consistently surrounded with positive, supportive energy, then commit to socializing more, connecting with co-workers or classmates, or joining professional groups to meet more people so you can build more beneficial relationships.

Gold Mind Mantras

- ◊ I am expanding my circle of friends.
- ◊ I am meeting people who can help me grow.

WHO IS YOUR INFLUENCE?

Who are you hanging out with? Who is giving you advice? Who is supporting you in your life journey?

I was once told that you are the sum of the five people you spend time with. If you have four broke friends, sooner or later you will be the fifth. The people around you are crucial, and they can either take you up or bring you down. You have to guard your time and your circle, and this includes family as well.

Oftentimes we come from cultures that believe blood is thicker than water. I would suggest weighing your options. If my cousin is a negative influence and doesn't support my journey, I should keep them at a distance. Conversely, my college roommate supports my journey and provides feedback and resources, so he should be someone I keep close.

Sometimes, our culture keeps us from moving forward because we are afraid to do something different than what our parents and grandparents have done. Maybe it's time to be a trendsetter, maybe it's time to move your family tree in another direction. We must not let the lack of exposure keep us in mental enclosures. Break the chains of your mind and surround yourself with people who are heading in the same direction.

What if your passion is helping others, volunteering at local churches and schools, giving back to the less fortunate, and reading books to seniors? But your co-worker is an introvert who likes to stay home by himself and watch Netflix and play video games? No one is right or wrong for doing what they love, but unfortunately, you both might keep your distance from one another because you have nothing in common besides work.

On the contrary, imagine the conversations you have with your best friend. How long do those conversations last? Likely hours. That person and you became the best of friends because of your similarities, not your differences. Positive relationships like these, that feed you, are worth nurturing and keeping.

Guard your heart and guard your mind. Your future self will thank you for this.

Also be mindful of who you're listening to. Is it the naysayers? Is it your disgruntled coworkers? Is it your unhappy family or friends? No matter who it is, when someone gives you advice, think about who they are as a person.

Is this a person who hasn't achieved many of their own goals and is miserable as a result? Is this someone who is cynical and critical, regardless of what good things come their way? If a person can't see and achieve success for themselves, it's almost impossible for them to see it for you.

We are all different. We might have similar backgrounds, but we have different experiences and environments. What we've seen is different and who we've spent time with is different. Consider this when someone you know gives you advice. Assume that every piece of advice they give you will be tainted by their own lived experience and their view on the subject.

Accept what they say with caution.

Gold Mind Work
1. Make a list of the top five people you spend time with. Are they motivating you toward your goals or holding you back?

Gold Mind Mantras
- ◊ I spend time with people who uplift me.
- ◊ I deserve to be surrounded by people who want to see me succeed.

GET A MENTOR

Having a mentor is like having a GPS to success. They provide resources, guidance, support, and motivation. A good mentor encourages, listens, inspires, provides corrective feedback, and is trustworthy.

When we start new careers or new positions, we need mentors to make us feel welcome and comfortable. A mentor is someone who can show us the ropes.

We can't do everything alone, and we can't think we know everything. It's okay to ask for help.

Finding a good mentor is essential for success. I have several mentors who are supportive, knowledgeable, and trustworthy. Each mentor serves a different purpose, and you have to identify their strengths.

If your career mentor isn't big on health and wellness, they might not be a good fitness mentor and vice versa.

It's very important to identify your mentor's strengths and weaknesses so you know what you can come to them for.

Gold Mind Work

1. Make a list of the areas in your life that you need mentorship in.

2. Identify who would be an ideal mentor in each area.

3. Reach out to them and ask for their help.

4. Show up for every conversation and opportunity! Be a good student. Mentors like people who value their time and take action on the advice and guidance they provide.

Gold Mind Mantra

◊ I am finding and attracting great mentors to guide me.

COACHING

Find a coach who can help guide you along the path you want to travel down. A coach should suit your personality and should not only be a mentor, but someone with experience in the field you are interested in. They should be able to give you direction, resources, and information you'd otherwise never knew existed. Your coach should listen, empathize, and give feedback.

You may think you can ask friends and family members to be your coach, but ideally, it needs to be someone you didn't know previously. Put simply, your friends and family know you too well to be honest and objective with you. A coach has to be someone who wants the best for you and is willing to give you tough love and criticism to grow and push you.

For a coaching relationship to work, you have to be *coachable*.

Everyone can learn something from anyone, including a child. Think about two babies from different cultures in one room. The first thing they would do is look at one another and start babbling, then they would run to one another and greet each other with a hug or a friendly smile. What we learn from these two beautiful souls is that our differences do not matter.

A great teacher was first a good student, and we must learn how to determine when to be a teacher and when to be a student. We teach when we are familiar with a subject, but sometimes we should listen with an open mind because it's time to learn.

I know being a student can make one feel less than, but we must understand learning is a part of life—no matter what age you are. Being a student doesn't mean you're lower than anyone; it means it's time for you to be exposed to something different and to learn something new.

It's okay to say "I don't know", but it's not okay to not look for the answer and refuse to learn. You used to be a student, but now you have the knowledge and understanding, you can become a teacher to someone. Don't be afraid to switch roles.

Remember, when we open our mouths, we tell the world who we are. Speak when you have authority or expertise on a topic. When you don't know, be willing to be a silent student.

Gold Mind Work

1. Find a coach who specializes in the area where you need the most growth and support in.
2. Contact them to discuss working together and what the investment (either time, money, or both) is.
3. Make the sacrifices necessary to work with them to elevate your life, performance, and potential.

Gold Mind Mantras

◊ I am coachable.
◊ I am open to learning what I don't know.

CREATE YOUR MASTERMIND GROUP

Simply put, a mastermind group is a group of like-minded people who come together regularly to discuss future and present goals with their peers and to guide one another to the next level.

A mastermind group is the perfect example of helping others and having others help you. A mastermind group exposes you to different cultures, experiences, and backgrounds. Forming a group with a diverse group of people increases your opportunities to really learn and benefit from each other.

You could either thrive or fail within this group, so you want to include the right people. To form a mastermind group, you need about three to five people. This might seem like a small number, but the bigger the group, the more opinions and less focus you'll have.

Also, members should be vetted. No, this isn't a job interview or a secret society, but it is an elite group of people coming together to make an impact. You decide what your vetting process will be—just make sure you choose the right people.

Your group can meet at a coffee shop, the library, or even rent a space. Set a schedule to get together regularly. Openly discuss successes and struggles, share valuable information, and be supportive of one another.

Always remember, we cannot get anywhere alone.

Gold Mind Work
1. Decide who you would like to invite to your mastermind group.
2. Reach out to each person to share your ideas for the group.
3. Determine the date, time, and location for your group to meet.
4. Create an agenda for your meetups.

Gold Mind Mantra
- ◊ I enjoy building and bonding with like-minded people.

ACCOUNTABILITY

Identify an accountability partner. It can be anyone, but make sure this person is aligned with your vision.

For example, Tommie is Ryan's accountability partner. Ryan is very goal-oriented and is clear on his vision for success. He is in graduate school for business and is building a tech startup.

On the other hand, Tommie has no goals for himself. He believes that playing the lottery every day will eventually lead to him becoming rich. Tommie is unemployed due to recent layoffs, but Tommie isn't worried about working because he is able to receive an unemployment check.

No shade to Tommie, but Ryan needs an accountability partner who understands his grind and hustle.

When choosing your accountability partner, choose someone who has a similar path and goals to your own.

Take your time selecting this person, because they are responsible for taking you to the next level. You should talk with them at least once a week, share your goals, and how you'll accomplish them. Your partner will check your progress and make sure you're on track. Oh, and you will be doing the same for them! True partnership goes both ways.

Gold Mind Work

Pick an accountability partner who understands your hustle, can help you reach your goals, and you can do the same for them.

Gold Mind Mantra
- ◊ I will be accountable to others, and I will hold others accountable.
- ◊ I see the value in accountability.
- ◊ I commit to accountability.

EXPECTATIONS

Many times, we expect more from others than what they cannot give us, which can leave us feeling negative and disappointed.

We are all guilty of expecting someone to do something a certain way and getting upset when they don't meet those expectations.

Try and meet people in the middle, and don't pressure them with high expectations, or else you'll struggle with finding that crucial positive attitude.

The only person you should set high expectations for is yourself.

Gold Mind Work

1. Where in your life are you holding people to expectations that are too high or unfair?

Gold Mind Mantra

◊ I release people of expectations.

Conclusion

I hope that you've learned a lot from this book. Some of the things you've learned will help you to connect better with the people you know and the people you'll meet along the way in life.

But, most importantly, I hope this book helped you learn how to connect better with the most important person that you know and will ever meet—you.

The person you are today is so drastically different from the person you will be one, five, ten, and twenty years from now. As you apply what you've learned in this book and grow, your life will completely change. You will be clearer, more focused, and more successful than you've ever been. But to make any of that happen, you need to know where you want to go in life and hold yourself accountable to getting there.

So, I want you to end this book by writing a letter to your future self.

Be very specific in this letter. This letter gives you purpose and direction. This letter will help you own your future and commit to what you say you're going to do.

Here are some questions to answer in your letter:

1. Who do I want to become?
2. What do I want to learn?
3. How much money do I want to make?
4. What type of person do I want to marry?
5. Do I want kids? How many kids do I want? What is my family's mission?
6. What type of car and house do I want? How many rooms? How many square feet?
7. What is your ideal weight goal?
8. What career do you want?
9. Where do you want to travel?

This is your life's vision. Put this letter away and remind yourself to read it ten years from today. Don't be surprised if you've accomplished more than what you wrote down or if you completed everything in less than ten years.

With everything you now know, your goals and dreams are accelerated. You can achieve more than you ever thought was possible. There is nothing that can stand in your way.

You have a Gold Mind—put it to work.

Additional Works from the Author
carmichaellewis.com

Shadows of the Past- *The Path to Greatness*

Julian Parker never prepared himself for the moment 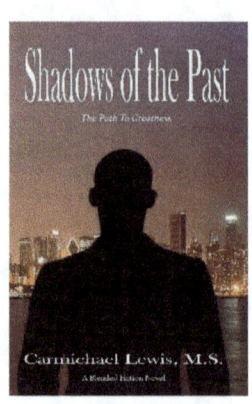 that this incredible woman would have walked into his life. Aniyah's presence captivated his soul from the second they met. By their first date, he knew she would be the perfect mate. People always mock love at first sight, but to Julian the disbelief was false. Julian had spent much of his adult-hood running from the past, fighting to free himself from the incidents that had plagued his life.

The newlyweds planned an incredible trip to Hawaii for their honeymoon, and it was an exhilarating time for both parties. Neither one had traveled much, so experiencing the event together made the trip all the more worthwhile. But then the unthinkable happened. Aniyah sat in a hospital room, watching an artificial machine breathe for her husband. The last thing she wanted was to think about traveling when the love of her life was in the hospital.

In the months that follow, joy takes over: Aniyah and Julian celebrate their incredible news. It's as if Julian's heart condition doesn't exist. They want to drag out the experience indefinitely. Julian feels alive for the first time in his life. In the midst of chaos, the couple finds happiness within the smallest package: a baby girl is on the way. As Julian faces the imminent possibility of death, it allows him to dig deep within his soul and confess the overwhelming events of his past. In return, he learns true love is unconditional.

The Ultimate Guide to Teenagers Success: *What They Don't Teach You in School*

The Ultimate Teenager's Guide; Transformation through self-education will educate young people on how to set goals to achieve their dreams, how to manage and save their money and how to stay mentally and physically healthy. With this book, it will help create a vision for their life and help them define what success looks like to them. As young as twelve years old, this book will inspire young people to discover their potential, teach them how to achieve financial independence, and how to succeed in school and beyond. This book will create a breed of healthy and wise adults who will protect the wellbeing of future generations. I sincerely believe that The Ultimate Teenager's Guide will change the trajectory of many teenager's lives for the better.

It is our responsibility as a society to guard the wellbeing of our children. This book is one essential tool that will affect the lives of young people and the community as a whole.

Mira Mira – Look!

Mira Mira-Look! shows how our household is teaching our son English and Spanish at the same time. By having a Hispanic mother and a black father, our son is learning how we are unique from traditional families.

Mira Mira- Look! teaches children a few common words they see daily. It introduces a second language and shows that children's curiosity sparks them to inquire about their environment... saying "Mira-Mira" in Spanish or "Look" in English. From our household to yours, we hope you enjoy Mira Mira-Look!

Daddy & Me

Daddy and Me is a gentle rhyming story told from the perspective of an adored baby boy. Follow Daddy and his son through their day together with your little one. Written intentionally with repetitive phrases and simple rhymes to engage your baby's attention and support cognitive development and recognition of routine.

Papá y yo

Papá y yo es un cuento de rimas desde la perspectiva de un pequeño bebé. Siga a papá y a su hijo en su día juntos y comparte las atrctivas y coloridas ilustraciones con tu pequeño. Escrito intencionalmente con frases repetitivas y rimas sencillas para captar la atención del bebé y apoyar el desarrollo cognitivo y el reconocimiento de la rutina.

Mamá y yo

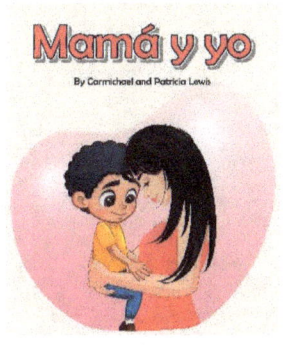

Mamá y yo es un cuento encantador desde la perspectiva de un hijo que describe las actividiades diarias que toman lugar en casa. Mamá y yo apoya el Desarrollo cognitivo de los niños con frases repetitivas y rimas simples' para llamar atención. Un libro perfecto para empezar el día.

Mommy & Me

Mommy and Me is a sweet story from the perspective of a son describing the daily activity that take place throughout their day. Mommy and Me support

children cognitive development with repetitive phrases and simple rhymes to engage their attention.

www.ingramcontent.com/pod-product-compliance
Lightning Source LLC
Chambersburg PA
CBHW071957070526
44583CB00015B/1236